Murder at the Front Door

By

John Tommasi

Author's Note

Certain names and locations have been changed to protect the privacy of a number of individuals.

Conversations and incidents have been recreated as accurately as possible, having been generated from witness interviews by the author, newspaper articles and police reports. A number of witness accounts, to no surprise, were contradictory and there is some artistic license in the recreation of conversations and events.

During the proof reading, some witnesses stated that a particular event didn't happen in the manner portrayed in the book, while others stated that it was exactly the way it happened. Any inaccuracies are mine.

The police reports were obtained as a result of a request for info in accordance with NH, RSA 91-A.

Dedicated to the memory of Mike Duggan of Salem, NH PD, and Miami-Dade Sherriff's Office; one of the original, and last, choir boys.

Acknowledgements

I would like to thank the following for taking the time to contribute, and be interviewed by the author: Jim Tuttle, Joe & John Galvin, Ann Towler, Steve Henderson, Mike Hureau, Katie Wentworth, Colon Forbes, Kathleen Hall and the entire Lane Library staff and thanks to Carolyn Fluke who gave me the idea for the title.

A very special thanks to Bill Lally, Bill Wrenn, Tim Collins and Bob Towler who were always there to answer questions on a nearly daily basis for nine months. Thank you to the reporters of the Hampton Union (especially Paul Wolterbeek) who's reporting of the case was complete and conclusive. Much of the exchanges in the trials of Sammi and Robert McLaughlin came from the Hampton Union.

As always, the biggest thanks goes to my wife Leslie who puts up with me and gives me her unconditional support.

Table of Contents

Prologue

June 1, 1988 7PM

Robert McLaughlin had just poured his third shot of vodka with a beer chaser. It was his fourth beer. He was sitting at the kitchen table of his small two bedroom apartment as he watched his neighbor, Robert Cushing Sr., get out of his car and walk into his house.

"Look at him, he has an ideal life, and I'm still a patrolman, all because of him. He doesn't deserve to be alive. It's because of him and his liberal son that I was never chosen for Detective or Sergeant."

****

December 12, 1955

Robert Randall and Fred Janvrin, both age 15, were best friends. After they came home from school they went to Janvrin's house in Salisbury, Ma, a border community with Seabrook, NH and a summer beach resort. Janvrin went downstairs to the cellar and came up with his father's 16 gauge, pump action shotgun and gave it to Randall who was at the top of the stairs. Unbeknown, to either teenager, the gun was loaded with double ought buck, 8 pellets with the approximate caliber of a .32, and the safety was off. Horsing around, Randall pointed the gun at Janvrin and pulled the trigger while saying "Pow." To his horror, the gun discharged with several pellets hitting Janvrin in the stomach and lower abdomen. After Janvrin fell down several steps and onto the cellar floor, Randall ran next door to a neighbor's house for help. The woman called 911 and then she and Randall ran back to Janvrin's house where she applied cold packs to Janvrin's head and tried to stop the bleeding. Janvrin was conscious at the time and Randall was hysterical and pleaded with Janvrin, "Not to die." In the follow-up investigation by police, Janvrin assured Randall that he would be ok and seemed to have no resentment about the shooting. Janvrin then became unconscious before the ambulance arrived, and died enroute to the hospital.

****

In a follow-up investigation by Salisbury police, the neighbor testified that she did hear the shot that killed Janvrin, but heard no yelling or any type of argument from the Janvrin home prior to the shooting. She also testified that Randall was highly emotional and collapsed after Janvrin was loaded into the ambulance. The parents of Janvrin expressed strong positive feelings towards Randall and stated that their son and Randall were the best of friends. They also stated that both boys never got into trouble despite the presence of several other boys with serious records living in the neighborhood. Police believed that both Janvrin and Randall hung out with the boys, but either did not participate in the trouble or were not caught.

However there was no doubt as to how upset Randall was over the death of his best friend. This was confirmed by the parents of both boys and Randall's teachers at school. This was not helped by boys at school who subsequently referred to Randall as "Killer" Randall for some time. He was also kidded by some delinquent boys that Randall, a murderer, was not going to prison while some of the other boys had done time in juvenile detention for less serious crimes, such as motor vehicle theft, kidnapping and robbery.

A Newburyport court judge ruled that that the shooting was a tragic accident and that Randall would do no time in juvenile detention but would undergo psychiatric counseling. A counselor determined that Randall was deeply troubled with survivor's guilt, and felt he had a need to be punished.

****

January 28, 1956

It was 5:40 PM when the boy walked into Dudley's Diner in Salisbury, Ma, about 1000 yards away from his home. He carried a double barreled shotgun that was not loaded.

"Is this a holdup," the waitress asked?"

The boy replied, "I guess so."

The waitress called another employee who recognized the boy and tried to talk him out of what he was doing. The boy told the waitress to give him the money in the register. She gave him $78. The boy replied that he only wanted half and gave her the money back. She counted out $39 and gave it to him. As he was leaving, one of the customers also tried to talk him out of it. The boy told the employees not to call the police until one-half hour after he left.

The boy went home, gave his stepfather the money, and told him that he wanted to turn himself in.

The waitress only waited 10 minutes before calling the Salisbury Police who went to the boy's house after responding first to the Diner. There, they spoke to the stepfather and placed the boy under arrest.

Robert Randall had satisfied his need to be punished.

****

Robert was subsequently convicted of robbery on February, 1956 and went to juvenile detention where he underwent weekly psychological counseling. In August of that year, the courts and probation department received a report from Samuel Harder, M.D., of Boston, Ma. In this report, it was noted that Robert had spent two weekends home with his family and no difficulty was reported; quite the contrary, it was a happy weekend for all, including Robert's siblings. It was also noted that people in Robert's community harbored no ill will towards him, including the parents of Fred Janvrin. The report concluded with the Doctor stating that Robert had attained the maximum benefit from the counseling and would further benefit by returning home while being on parole/probation.

Robert was subsequently released and returned to school. He wanted to start anew which included taking the name of his supportive stepfather. He was subsequently adopted by his stepfather and changed his name to Robert McLaughlin after he was released from probation in February 1958, and went on with his life.

****

October 1973

Bob McLaughlin had been a police officer in Hampton, NH for 3 years and was one of three officers, two patrolmen and a Sergeant, on patrol during the midnight shift, when he received a call to respond to Punky Merrill's Gun & General Store in Hampton Falls, NH. Hampton Falls is a small town just south of Hampton, NH with a population of 2000. Its police department consisted, at the time, of a full time Chief of Police and four special (part-time) officers. When the burglary alarm at the gun shop activated, it went to the Rockingham County Sheriff's office who covered for part-time police departments in the county when no one was on duty. The county's deputies were tied up at the time and Hampton and Seabrook PD's were contacted. Seabrook advised that they would have someone available shortly. In Hampton, Patrolman Kennedy and the Patrol Supervisor, Jim Kerns, were busy on a domestic dispute call, hence, McLaughlin was the lone ranger responding to the burglary alarm.

As McLaughlin arrived at the gun shop, he noticed three men coming out the side door, all carrying bags. The owner of the store, Punky Merrill, lived in an apartment on top of the Gun Shop & General Store, and when he saw McLaughlin pull up, he came outside carrying his shotgun. McLaughlin got out of the cruiser with his shotgun which was loaded with number four buckshot. McLaughlin yelled for the three men to stop or he'll shoot. Up until the mid-eighties, it was legal to shoot a fleeing felon in NH. As the three men fled across the driveway towards the woods, McLaughlin took a knee and fired (at the time, burglary at night of an occupied structure was, and still is, a class A felony). McLaughlin aimed at the hardtop about three feet behind the burglar. He had learned at the firing range that when you fire a shotgun at the hardtop or cement, the pellets would bounce up six inches and continue on their trajectory at that height. Several of the pellets hit the burglar in the legs. He was later identified as Richard Carson.

"Headquarters this is 307, send backup, I have three burglars and shots fired."

By this time, Hampton's other two units were enroute to back him.

"Seabrook PD to Hampton, I have two units on their way to that location."

McLaughlin ejected the spent round, which also caused another round to load. After checking the guy who was wounded for weapons, he started to run after the other two. He heard shots and felt bullets whistling past him. As it turned out, after McLaughlin fired his shotgun, Punky Merrill opened fire with his shotgun. Fortunately for McLaughlin, Punky's shotgun was loaded with lead slugs that were still in the gun since the end of last deer season, if he had double ought or bird shot instead, it was quite possible that McLaughlin could have been shot by Punky.

McLaughlin felt that one of the other two burglars fired shots at him but that was never proved.

Once he reached the woods, he stopped.

"Come on Bob, let's go after them," Punky said to McLaughlin. McLaughlin was a regular at Punky's store, like most local cops, they knew each other well.

"No, bad idea Punky, we got other units on the way, and if they see you with a gun, they may not recognize you and shoot."

"Yea, good point. I'll head back to the shop and turn on all the lights."

"Don't touch anything, we're gonna check for prints, and put the shotgun down."

"Gotcha."

When other units arrived they set up a perimeter and contacted State Police to see if they had a K9 unit available. Trooper Beaulieu, who was off duty at the time arrived about an hour after the call, and after a brief track through the woods, it ended at a dead end road where the burglars had probably left a car and subsequently fled.

The burglar who was shot, Richard Carson, was transported to Exeter hospital under guard. He was lucky. The one pellet that hit him went thru his calf without hitting any bone. He was released within 3 days and was eventually found guilty of burglary and sentenced to 2-4 years in county prison. He never gave up the names of his two accomplices.

However, John Paine was arrested after his fingerprints were found inside the store and he confessed. He also received 2-4 years in county prison. The third person was never found or identified.

Richard Carson subsequently sued the Hampton Police Department and Robert McLaughlin personally as a result of being shot by McLaughlin. To no surprise, this was a source of significant stress to McLaughlin which compounded the stress he was dealing with from the shooting. He firmly believed that he came close to dying. He was recently married and his first child was on the way. The Town of Hampton's insurance carrier stated that since the shooting occurred in Hampton Falls, they weren't responsible and would not provide coverage to the Town on this incident. As a result, the Town of Hampton told McLaughlin that he was on his own and they wouldn't cover him. Fortunately for McLaughlin, the Hampton Patrolmen and Sergeants had just formed a union, and their lawyer, Whitey Frazier, later to become the Honorable Judge Frazier, threatened an unfair labor practice in addition to suing the Town civilly. The Town eventually relented and provided legal counsel and monetary coverage to McLaughlin. The lawsuit brought by Carson was eventually dropped, but the entire event had left Bob McLaughlin significantly scarred. He received a commendation for bravery. It was given to him in the locker room one day before roll call. It didn't help.

****

April 29, 1974

It was 11:32 PM on a warm evening in May.
"Headquarters to 308."
"Ten-three," Robert McLaughlin answered.
"Go to 942 Woodland Ave, report of shots fired and a man down on the front lawn. Ambulance enroute."

Holy shit Robert McLaughlin thought and then answered, "ten-five."

"Headquarters to 312, can you back him?"

"Ten-five, responding code 2," Rick Mathews answered.

"Three-oh-five copied also, I'll be responding." Car three-oh-five was supervisor, Bill Ritchie.

"Headquarters to units, the ambulance will stage down the street from 942 and will respond once the scene is secured."

Four minutes later Bob McLaughlin arrived at the call.

"Headquarters I'm out, I got a man down and another with a handgun."

Damn Bill Ritchie thought, and he upped his response to code three. Rick Mathews did the same.

McLaughlin didn't think, he just reacted. He grabbed the cruiser shotgun and racked a-round in the chamber as he exited the cruiser and took cover behind the engine block.

"Drop the gun," he yelled to the man who was now standing over the body, "and put your hands on your head and walk towards me."

The man dropped the gun and started walking towards McLaughlin as Bill Ritchie arrived on the scene. Bill got out of the cruiser with his gun drawn. The shooter was later identified as Joe Williams who owned a bus company. While McLaughlin covered Williams, Bill handcuffed him.

"Three-oh-five to headquarters, have the ambulance respond. We've secured the scene and have one in custody. Tell the ambulance to step on it, the guy who's down is covered in blood."

"Ten-five."

Mathews arrived at the same time as the ambulance, and accompanied them to the man lying in blood. He was later identified as Robert Muller from Lexington, Ma.

The first EMT to arrive took one look at Muller and said, "He's gone."

"How do you know?" Mathews asked.

"The bullet hole right between the eyes has something to do with it. That gray stuff oozing out of his head is his brains. Not a thing we can do."

At this time, Katherine Williams, Joe's wife, came out of the house screaming.

Mathews and McLaughlin were able to take her into the house and calm her down. Detective Sergeant Norm Brown arrived on the scene and covered the body with a blanket that was in his unmarked car. The other patrolman on duty was Jim Tuttle who arrived on scene shortly after Brown.

"Jim, this is Joe Williams, he's under arrest for murder, transport him to the station and book him. It'll be McLaughlin's arrest," Bill Ritchie said.

"That the dead guy on the steps?" Tuttle asked.

"Yup, deader than a door nail, got him right between the eyes."

"That's cold," Tuttle answered as he was putting Williams in the cruiser.

Both McLaughlin and Mathews were able to calm Katherine Williams down and she was able to call her sister to come get her.

While they waited, they were able to get most of the story from her. Joe and she were going through a nasty divorce that just got nastier, and they were separated. At some point, Joe drove by the house and saw Muller's car in the driveway. Joe suspected Katherine was having an affair. Katherine surmised that Joe parked his car down the street and shot Muller when he came out of the house.

After Katherine's sister arrived, McLaughlin walked her to the car from the side door so she didn't have to see the body. He then came back to see Ritchie.

"Okay Bobby, you have the arrest. Tuttle transport Williams back to the station and dicks are processing the scene."

"Ok Sarge, I'll start right on the report."

"And Bobby, good job."

"Thanks."

It was McLaughlin's second gun incident in eight months.

Back at the station, Williams had already confessed to then Hampton Police Chief Clayton Bosquin who had been contacted earlier. Bosquin relayed the confession to McLaughlin.

"Williams said he and his wife had been separated and began seeing a marriage counselor in recent weeks, but that Muller continued to see his wife. He said friends and neighbors told him that Muller would come to the Woodland Road home after he had left for work."

Bosquin continued, "Williams then said after visiting with a friend, he drove by his house at around 11 when he saw Muller walking out the front door. He was holding the gun in his hand and pointing it at Muller's shoulder when Muller grabbed his hand and the gun went off. He didn't mean to shoot him, it was an accident."

After McLaughlin finished the report, he went home. It was 4 AM and he was still wound up from the night's incidents. He started drinking vodka with beer chasers.

McLaughlin was still drinking when Beverly, his wife, got up at 7 AM that morning.

"What the hell are you doing up and why are you drinking."

"I couldn't sleep. I went to a murder scene last night. Guy was shot right between the eyes. I saw his brains oozing out."

"I don't want to hear that. I'm making breakfast for Bobby jr. Deal with it and don't go talking to anyone at work. You don't want to lose your job. At least you got some overtime out of it."

Bob just looked at his wife. He went to bed and didn't get up until 5 PM that night, just in time to get ready for his 6-2 shift. He held everything in and didn't talk about it to anyone. The stress mounted for Robert. He received another commendation for his actions that night. This time it was in the roll call room.

****

Joe Williams was released the next day on $25,000 Surety bail. In other words, he put his house as collateral and walked out of jail. William's attorney, Richard Leonard, presented a letter to the court during a sanity hearing from a Boston psychiatrist who had examined Williams. Leonard quoted the doctor's letter as saying "Williams is not psychotic and not dangerous to himself and others."

His case went before a Grand Jury in June where they found no probable cause and the shooting was in fact an accident.

Charges against Joe were dropped and he and Katherine were eventually divorced.

****

August 17, 1975

Twenty-two year old Tim Campbell had just bought his Datsun 260Z and he couldn't believe how well it handled. It was a warm night and he had the T-tops off. What made it better was the gorgeous blonde Paula that was next to him in the passenger's seat. The night had gone well and as he was driving her home. He was hoping that she would invite him in. He was going a little too fast in his haste to get her home when he began to skid around a corner on Winnacunnet road. He overcompensated, began to fishtail and ended up in the oncoming lane. Luck was not with Tim and Paula that night. He hit a Dodge Swinger head-on as it was travelling in the opposite direction. Neither had their seatbelts buckled and both he and Paula hit the windshield. If anything good could be said, they died instantaneously.

****

"Headquarters to 307, respond to the area of 795 Winnacunnet Street for a 10-25 with PI, ambulance is enroute."

"Roger that headquarters, I'll be responding code 2," answered patrolman Robert McLaughlin.

Bobby, as he was called by his friends, had been on the Hampton, NH Police Department for 5 years. He was on his way to a serious motor vehicle accident with personal injury and he was going with blue lights and sirens. It was just before midnight.

"I copied that also, and I'll back him," stated then patrolman Rick Mathews. Rick and Bobby both got on the police department in 1970 and soon became close friends.

When Mathews and McLaughlin arrived at the accident site, they realized immediately that the accident was more serious than what the dispatcher indicated. It was a two car head on collision. They called for additional officers. They were joined by detective Tuttle and officer's Kennedy and Ritchie.

"Headquarters to units at the accident scene, two ambulances are enroute."

"Be advised," Rick Mathews responded, "we may not need them. This is a possible double 10-26," which was police code for a fatal accident. Rick called for additional units. Bill Wrenn, who was on a little more than a year, was one of the first units to arrive and he was immediately assigned to traffic control.

When the Hampton ambulances arrived on the scene, they confirmed the worst, it was a double fatal. They also called for a pumper truck to stand by as there was a gasoline leak from one of the cars involved in the accident.

The accident occurred in front of 795 Winnacunnet road, the Cushing residence. After being woken by the crash and subsequent arrival of emergency vehicles, Robert

Cushing Sr. dressed, lit a cigarette and went out his front door to see what was going on.

He walked to one of the victim's car while smoking and was advised by officer's Kennedy and McLaughlin to leave the accident scene and put out the cigarette since there was gas leaking from the cars.

"Oh, because you have a badge you can tell me what to do? I live here," replied Cushing.

McLaughlin stepped up and stated to Cushing, "Sir, if you don't put out that cigarette and move back, you'll be placed under arrest."

"You can't arrest me."

"I can and I will. Last warning sir. Either move or you'll be in handcuffs."

With that said, Cushing begrudgingly moved off the road and to his front yard.

A short time later, detective Tuttle began taking pictures of the accident. Cushing who was still steaming, from his recent encounter with McLaughlin, walked onto the road and in front of Detective Tuttle taking pictures.

"Sir, please move," said Officer Kennedy to Cushing.

"I will not move. You can't tell me what to do."

Officer McLaughlin was nearby. "Sir, you've been warned," and with that, officers McLaughlin and Ritchie placed Cushing under arrest and told him to place his hands behind his back.

"I will not. You can't arrest me."

A brief struggle ensued between Cushing and officer's McLaughlin and Ritchie. The struggle consisted of Cushing refusing to place his hands behind his back. After being assisted by Detective Tuttle, they were able to place the cuffs on Cushing and he was placed in the cruiser, transported to the station, and booked and bailed for disorderly conduct.

Bill Wrenn thought to himself that Cushing really tried hard to get arrested, and it appeared he succeeded.

When word of Cushing's arrest was circulated around town, everyone was amazed since they all felt it was out of character. He was a well-respected elementary school teacher. Cushing filed charges against the officers who arrested him and retained counsel to defend him. The charges against the officers were subsequently investigated and found to be without merit. There was eventually a negotiated plea to the disorderly conduct charge, which was continued for a year without a finding by Judge Gray at the District Court level. Essentially, a finding of continued for a year meant that if Cushing did not get arrested during the next year, the charges would be dropped.

****

September 23, 1975

It was a quiet Sunday morning in Hampton and 65 year old Gladys Ring was on her way to church when she rolled through a stop sign. Robert McLaughlin was on duty that day and was sitting on the side of the road observing traffic when Gladys went through the stop sign. After he pulled her over, Rick Mathews responded to back him.

"What do you have Bobby," Rick asked?"

"She blew a stop sign and she's upset that I stopped her. She won't give me her license." Both officers then approached the car.

"Mrs. Ring, if you don't give me your driver's license, we have no other choice but to arrest you and tow your car," McLaughlin said.

"I'm on my way to church, you have no right to stop me. I'm a grandmother."

"Ma'am, last time, if you won't give me your driver's license, you're going to be placed under arrest."
"You can't arrest me, my taxes pay your salary."
"Ma'am, step out of the car, you're under arrest."

"I am not," and with that Gladys locked her arms while grasping the steering wheel.

McLaughlin then opened the driver's door to the car and tried to pull her out of the car.

"Rick, give me a hand here, get her hands while I pull her out."

Both officers were then able to muscle Gladys out of the car but not before ripping the jacket she was wearing at the shoulder seem. She was transported to the station and charged with disobeying a police officer and resisting arrest. She was subsequently released on PR (personal recognizance) bail. Gladys Ring was the next door neighbor of the Cushings.

In a very short time, the story of Gladys Ring spread throughout the neighborhood and reached the ears of Robert Cushing Sr. and his son Renny. The Cushing's were outraged since the Cushing children and others in the neighborhood referred to Gladys as "Aunt Gladys".

The Cushing's, with Robert's arrest last month still fresh in their minds, started a petition within days that circulated throughout the neighborhood and Hampton condemning what they called the "aggressive tactics of the Hampton Police Department". They also demanded the termination of officer's Rick Mathews and Robert McLaughlin. The Cushing's went as far to appear before the Hampton Board of Selectmen to air their grievances.

After an internal investigation, both officers were cleared of any wrongdoing, and the petition went nowhere.

It seemed that everyone soon forgot about the incident, everyone except for Robert McLaughlin.

****

May 1, 1977

John Tommasi was a part-time police officer in Salem, NH, and even though he was finishing his Master's Degree in Business Administration in another year at the University of New Hampshire, he was seriously considering a career in law enforcement. It would have been a pay cut from his job at AVCO corporation (which was subsequently bought by Textron), but he was single, and money wasn't his primary concern in life. Going to a job he enjoyed was more important.

It was Sunday morning and he was doing fence duty at the construction site of the Seabrook, nuclear power plant. He was one of eleven Salem Police Officers who responded to the call for assistance from the Town of Seabrook. The newly formed Clamshell Alliance had over two thousand demonstrators surrounding the outside of the fence. They were anti-nuclear and their intent was to shut the site down.

Opposing them were two hundred and seventy police officers from all over New England. On fence duty with Tommasi was experienced NH State Trooper, Chris Colletti.

Looking at the demonstrators outside the fence, Tommasi said, "Hey Chris, doesn't this kind of remind you of the Alamo."

After a moment's hesitation Colletti turned to Tommasi and said, "Hey kid, ain't gonna fucking end like the Alamo."

"Good to know," Tommasi said nodding his head.

Later on that day, officers stationed at the Seabrook plant arrested over 1400 demonstrators in a mainly peaceful confrontation. Later on in life, Tommasi often wondered if Renny Cushing was one of the demonstrators he arrested.

****

April 1980

Bill Lally was a recent grad from Mt Wachusett College and he had just landed his dream job. He was a newly appointed patrolman in Hampton, NH. It was his third day on the job and he would be with a training officer for about four weeks. Today he would be working the 7 AM to 3 PM shift with newly appointed Sergeant, John Campbell. There was the usual roll call banter where new guys were the butt of the jokes and banter. The logic being, if you're thin skinned and can't take the roll call hazing, you certainly wouldn't make it on the street. All this hazing in the locker room and rollcall was referred to as the "Murderer's Circle" by Hampton Police Officers.

After roll call, John introduced Bill to Bob McLaughlin who was just coming back to work from two days off.

"Glad to meet you Bill. How do you like it so far and when are you going to the academy?" Bob asked.

"It's great! I have a lot to learn and it looks like I'll be going to the academy at Pease Air force Base in September."

"Well, you'll certainly learn a lot this summer. Hampton's population swells to over one-hundred thousand on some days, especially weekends," McLaughlin said.

"That's what I hear."

"Okay, enough of this, get in the car Bill, you're driving and your Sergeant wants a coffee," Campbell said kiddingly.

"Right Sarge. Nice meeting you Bob."

"You too Bill and good luck."

One of the things that Bill noticed was how immaculate McLaughlin's uniform was and he mentioned it to Campbell.

"His uniform was perfect. How does he get his boots like that?"

"It's called a spit shine. You'll have to learn that before you go to the academy. If not, plan on doing lots of pushups."

"Thanks. The Police Academy was recently increased to six weeks," Lally said.

"Yea I heard, when I went in 1974, it was only four weeks."

"Why is the academy at Pease?"

"They have army barracks that you stay in and cafeteria facilities. They'll be building a new academy in Concord, but it probably won't be ready until eighty two. And by the way, the barracks are drafty, so you're lucky you not going in the winter, and the food sucks. On the plus side, you get to come home on weekends," Campbell answered.

"Got it."

"And by the way, if you want to model yourself after anyone, it's Bob McLaughlin. His uniform is always impeccable, and besides his shoes, he shines his brass every day. He's proud of the way he looks and the job he does. He's a real cop's cop, and his nickname is the Mongoose.

"Why's that?"

"Because like a mongoose, he always gets his quarry. He is relentless if he's investigating a crime, and his DWI reports are spot on. He's been in shootouts and high speed chasers and murder scenes. He has never lost a high speed pursuit and he's probably the best driver and shot in the department. He is the man"

"Thanks sarge, and that's not the first time I've heard that."

"Okay, coffee Lall."

Throughout his career, Lally was known as Lall.

****

Summer 1983

John Tommasi had been on Salem, PD for four years full-time, and had just made patrol Sergeant. He had recently started a business, Sub Sea Salvage, where he taught and certified Suba Divers and did underwater salvage work. After certifying eight members of the Salem, NH Fire Department, they were doing additional training with him on search and recovery.

Today, Tommasi was freelancing for an insurance company. He was diving in the Merrimac River recovering stolen cars that were driven off the boat ramp in Lawrence, Massachusetts, just north of the dam. There were two gangs in Lawrence that were responsible for the stolen cars, The *Southside Kings* and *License to Steal*. They would typically steal a high performance car, try to get in a pursuit with any of the local police departments, including Salem, NH, and then drive them off the boat ramp into the murky waters of the Merrimac. Lawrence had the unflattering moniker of stolen car capital of the United States.

Tommasi knew that the Merrimac was heavily polluted and over fifty thousand gallons of raw sewage was dumped into the river daily from Manchester and Nashua, NH. The EPA was just beginning to take measures to clean the river. In order to safely dive in the river, Tommasi had gotten a tetanus and gamma goblin shot to protect him from hepatitis A. He was also wearing a dry suit and full face mask.

This was Tommasi's first car he was diving on and he wasn't surprised that he had zero visibility. He located the car by the oil slick that was rising from the engine, followed it down 15-20 feet and attached the hook from a tow cable to one of the axels of the car. After surfacing, he would signal the tow truck driver who would winch the car out. He recovered sixteen cars that summer.

He was off that day and that night he spent at his beach cottage that he rented that summer on M street in

Hampton with four other Salem cops who were all recently divorced. Tommasi, at thirty, was the only one who was still single. They were sitting on the farmer's porch at 11:30 PM, on the front of the cottage, when they were joined by Bob Mark, Bill Wrenn and Bob McLaughlin who just got off duty from Hampton.

"Hey, we heard you guys are having a choir practice," Bill Wrenn said.

"Yes we are," answered Tom Ferris one of the recently divorced Salem cops.

"And we have plenty of choir books for you guys too," said Mark Cavanaugh who was also recently divorced. Bottles of beer were passed around.

"Hey Tommasi, I heard you were diving in the Merrimac today," Wrenn said.

"Yea, I was contacted by an insurance company to recover stolen cars in Lawrence."

"No shortage of those. How's the visibility?" Mark asked.

"What visibility? I literally couldn't see my hand in front of my face. There's shit floating everywhere in that river, and once I stepped on the bottom, my foot sank a foot into the silt"

"I hope they're making it profitable."

"That they do. I'm getting $100 for each car. Today was my first and I've got another dive scheduled in a couple of days."

"Doesn't Lawrence use the Merrimac for drinking water?" McLaughlin asked.

"Yea they do. They must purify the hell out of it. But I'm not drinking it."

"Now that you mention it, I won't either."
McLaughlin said. The fact that the Merrimac was highly
polluted and silted stayed with McLaughlin over the years.
*Authors note: When cops get together after work and have
a few drinks, it's known as choir practice. The bottles are
referred to as choir books, and of course, the cops who are
drinking, are called choir boys. It is believed that this
practice was started in LA and was made popular by
Joseph Wambaugh's 1975 book, The Choir Boys.*

****

April 5, 1986

It was the 1st week in April and the busy summer
season in Hampton was beginning. April and May could
be busy months depending on the weather, especially on
weekends and it was an usually warm Saturday night in
Hampton. Some people were taking long weekends and
some of the college kids who had summer jobs in Hampton
were beginning to show up.

Joe Galvin had just finished his rookie year and was
glad to be off probation. It was 9 PM and Joe was sitting in
his cruiser at the intersection of Ocean Blvd and Ashworth
Ave, referred to as AshCor by members of the police
department. He was watching both pedestrians and
vehicular traffic. It was a fairly busy Saturday night when
he heard a general announcement from dispatcher Mary Jo
Ganley.

"Headquarters to all units, be on the lookout for a
dark colored, older model Oldsmobile, with possibly Maine

license plates, traveling north on Ocean Blvd from O street. One male subject driving, possible 10-19," 10-19 being police code for driving while under the influence.

Joe heard the call.

"Headquarters this is 306, I'm at Ashcor and I'll keep a lookout for it." Ashcor was about one-half mile north of O Street on Ocean Blvd. Ocean Blvd was a two lane road with one way northbound traffic. Ashworth Ave was for southbound traffic. Ashcor was the where the two roads became adjacent to each other.

Within minutes, Joe spotted the car.

"Headquarters, this is 306, I have a car and driver matching that description travelling north on the Blvd. I'll be stopping him."

"Headquarters to units, anyone in the area for backup."

Robert McLaughlin was in the station. He had just finished cleaning his handgun. In 1986, Hampton Police, like most other departments in New Hampshire carried the Smith & Wesson .357 magnums as a sidearm and every cruiser had a shotgun with double ought buck for ammo.

"Headquarters this is 308, I'm just clearing the station. I'll head that way." The police station was about ¼ mile from Joe's location.

"Headquarters, I'm attempting to stop that vehicle northbound on Ocean Blvd, he isn't speeding up, just not stopping, speed about 35. Be advised, he's all over the road," Joe Galvin radioed as he caught up to the Oldsmobile.

Upon hearing this, McLaughlin activated his blue lights and siren attempting to close the gap.

Rick Mathews, a recently promoted Sergeant was the supervisor that night.

"Headquarters, this is 305, I'm on Winnacunnet Rd east of the high school. I'm heading that way." Winnacunnet road was north of Joe's position and intersected Ocean Blvd.

"Headquarters this is 306, I have him stopped at the Century motel. He pulled into the driveway." The Century was on a section of Ocean Blvd referred to as Rocky Bend and had a horseshoe driveway with individual units lined around the drive. Joe had the car stopped in front of the second unit on the right. He parked his cruiser at an angle to the stopped Oldsmobile to offer some protection as he was taught at the academy.

"Joe, I'll be there in a minute," McLaughlin radioed.

"Me too," Rick Mathews echoed.

As Joe Galvin approached the driver's door of the Oldsmobile, he was able to smell alcohol coming from the driver, later identified as Ken Woodward, a Viet Nam Vet.

"Sir, can I have your license and registration and why didn't you stop for me," Joe asked.

"I had the radio up loud and I didn't notice you," Woodward replied.

As Woodward was talking, the odor of alcohol became stronger and Joe noticed how his speech was slurred and eyes were bloodshot. All good indicators of a drunk driver.

Joe went back to his cruiser and ran Woodward for a valid license. He came back under suspension for a previous DWI conviction. Hmm, Joe thought, the best judge of future behavior is past behavior

As Joe was exiting his cruiser, he noticed the driver, the only occupant, bend down and either put something under the seat, or take something out, he couldn't tell. This is what most police officers refer to as furtive movements which instantly put Joe on alert. As he approached the stopped Oldsmobile, Joe unsnapped his holster and put his hand on his .357. When he reached the driver's door, he stood back forcing Woodward to turn almost 180 degrees. As Joe was about to ask him to exit the car and perform some field sobriety tests, Woodward pulled a gun, a Ruger Bulldog .44 magnum with a 2 ½ inch barrel. As Woodward turn, he fired at Joe, missing him. Joe returned a shot which missed Woodward and lodged in the steering wheel column. Galvin and Woodward were about three feet apart. Galvin retreated to his cruiser and he radioed that he's in a gunfight.

The Bulldog has a 5 shot capacity and Woodward quickly emptied his gun shooting at Joe missing him with every shot. Joe returned fire, shot for shot, also missing Woodward, but he saved the last bullet in his revolver, he didn't know that Woodward's gun is empty. Woodward then backed his car around Galvin's cruiser at the same time McLaughlin arrived on the scene from the south and Mathews from the north.

McLaughlin and Mathews both exited their cruisers with shotguns. As Woodward backed out of the driveway and began to head north on Ocean Blvd, McLaughlin fired a shot through the rear window completely shattering it, and as he attempted to eject the spent cartridge, his shotgun jammed. All eight .32 caliber pellets missed Woodward.

Mathews had pulled into the other side of the horseshoe driveway and as Woodward drove by him, he fired his shotgun at Woodward through the front passenger's side window shattering it. Mathews was kneeling down and shot at an upward angle, all eight of his .32 caliber pellets missed Woodward, with most of them going through the roof of the Oldsmobile. All three officers got back in their cruisers and gave pursuit along with Officer Lee Griffen who arrived at this time and was behind McLaughlin.

"Headquarters we're in pursuit northbound on Ocean Blvd, multiple shots fired. Contact North Hampton and Rye," Mathews screamed over the police radio.

Woodard took off northbound on Ocean Blvd with all four officers in pursuit.

"My shotgun jammed. If we start shooting again I'll be on my magnum," radioed McLaughlin.

"Sarge if I have the shot, can I shoot," radioed Griffen who was still in his rookie year."

"Hell yes," answered Mathews.

The pursuit continued north on Ocean Blvd.

"Ok, he's turning onto High street from OB, he could be heading for route 101 or 95, contact NH State Police," Mathews advised dispatch.

"Already did sarge," answered Mary Jo.

"Mass State police has been advised also."

"We're coming up on route 1," Continued Mathews. What's common in many police pursuits is that the lead pursuit car, which was Joe Galvin, concentrate on driving while the second car in the pursuit, Mathews, called in locations. Route 1, also known as Lafayette road was the main north-south road in Hampton. There was usually a traffic bottleneck at the intersection of High street where there were stop lights. Woodward blew through the red light almost causing an accident. All four cruisers had their lights and sirens on which gave motorists some warning as they went through the intersection.

In another mile, Woodward turned onto route 101 west and from there, route 95 south barreling through a toll booth with four Hampton units and one NH state unit following which was waiting for them at the toll. This was radioed to Hampton Dispatch by Mathews.

"Headquarters to units, be advised, there are two Mass state units at the state line, they're planning on doing a rolling roadblock to try and slow them down, they are monitoring us."

"Units copy. We're about ½ mile north of the state line doing around 80-100. He's all over the road," Mathews replied.

A rolling roadblock occurs when multiple police units get in front of the vehicle being pursued and slowly reduce speed thereby slowing the chase, while other units box him in from the side and back.

"We're coming up on the state line and Mass state units are moving."

Since there were only two units, Woodward slowed slightly before flooring the pedal getting by the Mass state units while sideswiping one in the process.

"He's by the state units and he hit one as he was passing it. Pursuit is continuing south on 95 south, we're just south of the 495 intersection," Mathews radioed.

As the pursuit continued southbound on 95, the Mass state units tried to get past Woodward, but every time they did, he attempted to swerve into them.

"Mass 517 to base, I just want to confirm, this subject we're chasing fired shots at a cop."

"That's affirmative 517," Mass State Police dispatch answered.

"Okay, once I get pass the Whittier Bridge, I'm ending this."

"Base copies"

Mass State Trooper Richards was a 10 year veteran of the state police and had been in his share of pursuits. Pursuit policies in the eighties in both Mass and New Hampshire were much less restrictive than current pursuit policies.

As Woodward went over the bridge, Richards pulled alongside of him on the left. Woodward tried swerving into Richards, which he avoided. Richards responded by hitting Woodward's left rear quarter panel with the front right fender of his cruiser causing Woodward's Olds to spin out onto the median strip. Woodward tried running away, but was tackled. He resisted, was eventually subdued after a struggle, placed in handcuffs and transported to Newburyport, Mass PD. He was subsequently extradited to NH for trial where he was found not guilty by reason of insanity and sentenced to the state mental hospital. He was not released until 2017. All officers and Troopers involved in the shootout and subsequent pursuit received commendations and returned to work.

Chapter 1

Murder in the Neighborhood
Wednesday, June 1, 1988

Detective Bill Lally was an 8 year veteran of the Hampton Police department and was watching the Celtics playoff game against the Detroit Pistons when he got the call from Dispatcher Fred Ruonala around 8:45 PM.

"Bill there's been a homicide at 795 Winnacunnet Street, they need you there."

"Did you say a homicide?" Bill replied. In his eight years as a Hampton police officer, there had not been a single murder, and the only time officers had to deal with a dead body during that time was usually a result of a car accident or untimely death.

"Yea, that's right, it looks like two shotgun slugs to the chest. Guy died on the spot. His name is Robert Cushing," Fred responded.

"On my way."

Bill told his wife Sandy where he was going, kissed her goodbye, and was out the door

The Cushing family was known to Bill and most of the Hampton Police Officers. Robert Sr. was well known in the Community, and Bill was aware that Cushing had previously been arrested for disorderly conduct. He also knew of his son Renny (Robert Jr.) Cushing who tried to get Rick Mathews and Bobbie McLaughlin fired for the arrest of Gladys Ring. He, and other officers, had also been to the Cushing house a number of times on loud party calls.

There were seven children in the family and they were never really excited to see the police, especially given their father's previous interaction with the police.

Bill arrived at the house after first getting his gear at the police station and parked his cruiser adjacent to the yellow crime scene tape. As he walked into the house, he noticed two large bullet holes in the screen door and an enormous pool of blood coagulating on the inside hallway.

The victim, Robert Cushing, had been taken to Exeter Hospital via ambulance. He was very obviously dead at the scene because of blood loss and internal organ damage from two massive holes in his chest and abdomen, but because his wife was hysterical by that time, they felt it best that they transport him.

From the size of the holes in the screen door, Bill knew that they had to come from two shotgun slugs. He then noticed that there were no spent cartridges on the floor or outside the front door. After asking the uniformed officers present if they had seen any spent cartridges and getting a negative reply, he reasoned that the shooter had either policed his brass, or a double barreled shotgun was used which had to be broken open to eject the spent casings. Upon further observation, he saw no obvious clues. It was going to be a long night.

Authors note: Policing the brass is the phrase that is used to pick up spent cartridges after a gun is fired.

****

Fifteen minutes earlier

Marie Cushing, an avid basketball fan, was at home watching the Celtics playoff game like many people in the Boston area. Her husband, Robert, was across the living room sitting in an easy chair reading the newspaper while having a cocktail.

"I don't believe you're not watching the game," Marie said.

"You're the basketball fan, I'm enjoying just relaxing and being here with you," Robert replied.

"Come here and sit with me and watch the game. You can read the paper later."

As Robert got up to join his wife on the couch, there was a knock on the door.

"You're going to get that, right," Marie asked?

As Robert opened the front door, a momentary look of horror crossed his face as two blasts rang out through the still closed screen door driving the 63 year old Cushing back before he hit a hallway table. Marie screamed and rushed to her husband's side.

****

Hampton, NH is a relatively sleepy seaside community of 15,000 people that is just north of the Mass, NH border. However, in the summer, the town's population surges to well over 100,000 as people flock to the beachside resort for day trips and extended vacations. This often taxes the police force of thirty four full time officers and seventy part-time officers who often work a full time schedule during the summer. During the summer months, it is not uncommon to have over 30 officers on cruiser and foot patrol on an evening shift, particularly on weekends. The busy nights of the week were obviously weekends and also Wednesday nights because of weekly fireworks display.

Fred Ruonala, a dispatcher and communications specialist, was a 9 year veteran of the police department when he received the call.

"Hi, this is John Smith, my daughter and I just heard what sounded like two gunshots coming from our next door neighbor's house, the Cushing's."

Tim Collins was a five year veteran of the police department when he received the call from dispatch a little after 8:30 PM.

"Headquarters to 311, respond to the area of 795 Winnacunnet reference a report of two 10-66's," police code for shots fired.

Tim responded, "10-5, enroute."

Laura Stoessel, also a five year veteran, responded.

"Headquarters, this is 308, I'm in the area. I'll slide that way too."

The Wednesday night fireworks display wasn't scheduled to start for another two weeks Tim thought, so the reported shots could've come from a car backfiring or from a neighbor lighting off personal fireworks.

Tim and Laura arrived at the Cushing house at about the same time and parked across the street using their cruisers as cover. In the 80's, most police departments didn't require their officers to wear bullet proof vests, but in Hampton, they had them in their cruisers. Both officers went to their trunks and put them on.

At this time, on duty detective, Phil Russell arrived on the scene.

"Tim, I'm going to go down the road a bit and check out the woods by Presidential Circle to see if it's someone target shooting," Laura said.

"Ok," Tim replied.

"Phil and I will check out the area."

****

Leslie and John Campbell had been high school sweet-hearts and were married shortly after college. They lived on Presidential Circle which was a side road off of Winnacunnet road, about 50 yards east of the Cushing home and on the opposite side of the road. John was on a rare night off, since he liked to work overtime, and he was at a friend's house in Seabrook with some other cops watching the Celtics/Pistons playoff game. Leslie was a nurse and he was a Police Sergeant in Hampton. Nurses and cops were generally a good fit. Leslie had just put her two young children to bed in the upstairs bedroom when she heard two shots. Her neighbor, Charles Peters, owned Meadow Pond Farm, a large farm which included a heard of sheep which was adjacent to the Campbell land. Peters had told Leslie that either a fox or coyote was killing his sheep at night and he was going to stay up late this night to try and kill "the varmint," so if she heard a shot, not to worry. At that time, the area around Presidential Circle was primarily rural and undeveloped. Leslie figured that Peters ended his varmint problem.

****

As Tim and Phil approached the Cushing's front door, Phil noticed the door was open and the screen door closed. As they got closer Phil asked, "Are those two bullet holes in the front door?"

"Holy shit," Tim responded and saw someone lying in the hallway over a two foot tall table with his enthralls hanging out of his abdomen. He called dispatch for an ambulance and told them to step on it. Tim then saw a person further down the hallway and announced, "Hampton Police, please come out."

The person is Marie Cushing, and all she could see was Detective Phil Russell who was in plain clothes. Fearing that Phil may be the shooter. She called the police station.

"My husband's been shot."

Fred Ruonala was amazed at how calm she was, but like Bill Lally, during his tenure at Hampton, there was never a homicide.

"With a gun?" he asked somewhat amazed.

"Yes, through the front door," she answered.

"Please send help and an ambulance and there are people outside my front door."

After ascertaining the caller's name and she's at the same location as his officers, he called the fire department for an ambulance and advised the officers on scene that this is a possible 10-54. He also calls senior detective Bill Lally.

Stephen O'Connor, a rookie part time officer was riding with 4 year veteran officer, Steve Henderson.

"What's a 10-54," he asked.

"Damn," Steve replied.

"That's a homicide."

Steve turned on his lights and siren and headed towards the scene.

"Headquarters to 305, did you copy?"

"Enroute," responded Sergeant John Galvin (Joe's older brother), the street supervisor.

****

After hearing the 10-54 call, Tim approached the door where he was in full sight of Marie Cushing. Marie ran hysterically into Tim's arms sobbing, "They killed him."

By this time Laura was back on the scene and began to comfort Marie Cushing who was beginning to sob uncontrollably, while Tim and Phil entered the house. The ambulance, which came from the Fire Department a mile down the street, arrived on the scene and the two fireman started to administer to Robert Cushing while Tim and Phil cleared the house and determined that there was no one else present.

One of the ambulance medics checked Robert Cushing, and announced to Tim, "We got nothing here, here's gone and started to leave."

Officer Collins relayed this to dispatch, and dispatcher Fred Ruonala called the Fire department's battalion commander and convinced him that they need to transport the body to the hospital because of the hysterical Marie Cushing. This was relayed to the medics on scene and they placed the body in the ambulance and left the residence heading towards the hospital.

Henderson and O'Conner had arrived on the scene and O'Conner was tasked with accompanying Cushing's body to Exeter hospital. It was the first time he had seen a dead body, let alone a dead body riddled with two shotgun slugs.

By this time, Officer Stoessel was able to have dispatch contact the Cushing's oldest son, Robert Cushing Jr., known as Renny, who arrived to comfort his mother while grieving himself.

****

About fifteen minutes after hearing the two shots, Leslie Campbell's phone rang.

"Leslie, it's Sandy Lally, lock your door right away. I know you always leave it open."

"Why, what's going on?"

"Bill just got called in. There's been a murder right down the street."

"What?" Leslie like everyone else thought that was incredulous.

"It looks like someone shot this guy twice."

"Oh my God. I heard the two shots. Ok I have to go lock the doors and call John."

"Ok, be careful Leslie."

Leslie couldn't believe that there was a murder in her neighborhood. She ran downstairs and locked the front door. She then ran to her room and got a .38 police revolver from the lock box and loaded it. Like most cop's wives, she knew how to shoot and was comfortable around guns since John had taken her to the range a number of times. She then sat outside her children's bedrooms and called John at his friend's house from the upstairs hallway phone.

"John it's for you. Your wife."

"John, I just got a call from Sandy Lally. Bill's been called in. There's been a murder down the street on Winnacunnet. I heard the shots."

"Lock the doors," John answered.

"Already did and I have the police special and I'm outside the kids room."

"Alright, I'm on my way home. When I get home I'll honk the horn and call out it's me, so don't shoot."

"Okay."

As John hung up, everyone's beeper went off. It was going to be a long night.

****

Detective Sergeant Mike Simmons who was off duty, just happened to be in the police station when the call came in. He arrived at the Cushing house and instructed officers to put yellow crime scene tape around the house and curtilage. Officer Tim Collins was tasked with logging who went into the crime scene and who went out and what time. While Sergeant Simmons, Phil Russell and Bill Lally, who just arrived, began processing the crime scene inside the house, Patrol Sergeant Galvin began to organize a search of the scene with officers Henderson and three other Patrolman who arrived on the scene.

Just to the right of the Cushing house was a three story apartment complex with a paved parking lot behind it. The Cushing's had a large back yard that extended back to a wooded area.

"Okay Steve, you and Stoessel stay on my right and Jones and Kerry on my left. Make sure you have your vests on and a flashlight. We're going to search the backyard into the woods and we're looking for evidence. Anything out of the ordinary, sing out. I don't think the shooter is here, but be careful. Does everyone have their vest on?" Sergeant Galvin asked. After receiving affirmatives, the search started.

While Galvin was doing this, Chief Bob Mark arrived on scene and was logged in by Tim Collins who brought him up to date. To Bob Mark's credit, he let his detectives run the scene and he stayed back and overseered the work done by his officers. He was happy with what he was seeing. Even though it was the first homicide for most of them, everything was being done right.

****

When Bill Lally arrived, and was recorded in by Officer Collins, he spoke to his Sergeant, Mike Simmons.

"Hi Lall, Cushing's wife saw pretty much the whole thing. Her son Renny arrived, and took her to his house. She didn't get a look at who did the shooting."

"We got anything to go on," Bill asked?

"So far, we got nothing outside of the two shotgun slugs, through the screen door."

"Okay, by the numbers then," Bill responded.

Just then, the Hampton Police paddy wagon arrived on the scene. Tonight, it was also doubling as a crime scene van and the two officers who were in it began unloading lights on a stand that were place around the house and back yard to augment the spotlights and ally lights from the cruisers.

As this was happening, Detective Shawn Maloney and Deputy Chief Bill Wrenn arrived at the house. Bill Wrenn was the Deputy Chief in charge of investigative services and after he received the call of a homicide, he was thinking the person who did it was a family member which typically happens in a domestic situation. Bill also thought that this was the first homicide in Hampton since 1974, fourteen years earlier.

"You're not going to believe this," Bill Lally said.

"Somebody shot Richard Cushing Sr. through his front door. He's dead and the body has been removed."

"Anyone else home or see anything," Deputy Chief Wrenn asked.

"Not a thing. His wife Marie was watching the Celtics game and all she saw was Cushing falling back through the hallway after two loud blasts, her words. It was probably a shotgun loaded with slugs by the size of the holes in the screen."

"Okay you, Shawn and Mike handle the scene, I'll be with Chief Mark, and remember guys, you just have one shot to do a good job at a crime scene," and with that, Wrenn let his men do their job.

The three detectives split duties. Bill started processing the door and began looking and dusting for fingerprints. He knew that tomorrow he would have to interview Marie Cushing and take elimination prints. That would be anything but pleasant. As he looked at the door, he noticed that one of the shotgun slugs, after going through the screen, took a chunk out of the door, which told him that Cushing had either not opened the door all the way or he had tried to close the door after he saw the assailant with a shotgun. He would have to find out if Cushing yelled or said anything prior to the shots. In looking at the two shots, it appeared that one may have gone into his stomach and another into his chest. As he started to dust the door and screen door for fingerprints, he thought to himself he would have to get the coroner's report.

Shawn Maloney started looking in the front yard of the house and immediate vicinity. He was looking for anything the killer may have left behind or footprints which would have given investigators some indication to his physique. He found nothing, absolutely nothing. He then turned his attention to the backyard.

"Hey Shawn," Sergeant John Galvin called out.

"The backyard is gonna be contaminated. Me and the guys walked through it. We found nothing and then we searched the woods."

"Okay, thanks John. If you guys didn't find anything, there's probably nothing, I'm just going to give it a walk through."

****

Shawn and Bill finished about the same time when they got together to process the inside of the house. As they were about to start, Deputy Chief Wrenn waved them over.

Barbara Keshen had just arrived. She was one of the assistant NH Attorney Generals and she was responsible for the handling of the murder investigation and any subsequent prosecution of a perpetrator(s). She was appointed to the position in 1985 by Attorney General Stephen Merrill who was still in office and had been appointed by then Governor John Sununu. State Police Lt. Dan Lenihan was also on scene. In 1988, State Police had jurisdiction of any murder investigation in any municipality under 3000 people. If the population was over 3000, the Chief of Police of the municipality could conduct his own investigation or relinquish it to State Police. Bill Wrenn advised Dan that Hampton would conduct the investigation and if they needed anything, they would call. Hampton PD and State Police had a very good relationship and worked well together, especially during the busy summer months at Hampton.

The relationship with Barbara Keshen was different. For an Assistant AG, her view of police seemed to be jaundiced, and Hampton Police felt that her view of local police departments was less than warm.

When Keshen arrived on the scene, she asked Bill Wrenn who was conducting the investigation, Hampton or State Police.

"We are," Bill answered.

Bill then noticed a frown and look of displeasure on Keshen's face.

"Will you be running it Chief Wrenn?" It is common to refer to a Deputy Chief as Chief.

"I'll be overseeing it," Wrenn answered.

"And Detective Sergeant Mike Simmons will be running it with his two detectives, Bill Lally and Shawn

Maloney," and with that, Wrenn motioned Mike Simmons over.

Mike was talking to Bill Lally on the front porch and they both walked towards Keshen.

Mike had been a Sergeant for 4 years at the time and was just recently assigned as Detective Sergeant. He had spent his eighteen years as an officer in patrol, and as a result, had limited investigative experience.

"Mike, Bill, this is Barbara Keshen from the AG's office. She'll be handling the investigation and prosecution."

Keshen wasted no time, "So tell me Sergeant, what have you done and what will you be doing?"

Simmons hesitated for a moment and then said, "Well, we'll be doing the whole nine yards."

Keshen looked at him for a moment.

"Please tell me, what's the whole nine yards?"

At this point, Bill Lally saw Simmons foundering and jumped in.

"Well Barbara," Lally said.

"We've already completed a walk through the house and searched the front and back yards hoping to find something, especially footprints or maybe pieces of clothing, but no luck. Patrol Sergeant Galvin and some patrolmen walked the woods. No luck there either. The only evidence we have so far is the screen door with two holes in it. By the size of the holes, we're pretty confident that it was from two shotgun slugs."

Keshen was about to ask a question, but Lally continued.

"There were no ejected casings, so the shooter either policed his brass or it was a doubled barreled shotgun. I've already fingerprinted the front door and screen door and we have some prints. But we need to get elimination prints from the family. So far, all we have for evidence is the door. We'll be interviewing family members and friends during the following days and try to get a suspect. In addition, we'll be talking to neighbors. We've also photographed the entire scene."

Keshen nodded her head.

"Would you like to walk the perimeter," Wrenn said to Keshen."

"Yes please."

Ten minutes later they were finished.

As they were walking to the front of the house, Renny Cushing pulled up to the front of his parent's house. Bill Wrenn knew Renny and made introductions.

"Renny, this is Barbara Keshen from the AG's office, she'll be coordinating the investigation from the AG's office and handling the prosecution once we've made an arrest."

"I'm very sorry for your loss, and we'll be doing everything humanly possible and we'll get the person who did this," Keshen said. She didn't know this, but it was the beginning of a long, friendly political relationship with Renny Cushing which would be full of mutual respect.

"Glad to meet you too. I have no idea who would've done this."

"How's your mom doing?" Wrenn asked.

"How do you think," Cushing answered.

Generally, Wrenn would have had a response, but let it pass under the circumstances.

Keshen then stepped in and gave Renny her card and told him he could call anytime. He left shortly thereafter and Keshen walked backed to Deputy Chief Wrenn.

"All right Chief, if there's nothing else, I'll be leaving, please keep me in the loop."

Wrenn assured the Assistant AG that she would be kept in the loop. She left shortly thereafter just as the first of the news media arrived, the New Hampshire TV station, WMUR.

"She's a real joy," Simmons said.

Wrenn just nodded his head and smirked.

"Mike, you head to the hospital and try and get the slugs for evidence. Also check to see when the autopsy will be, one of us will have to be there," Wrenn said.

"Will do Chief," and he headed towards his cruiser.

Luckily Chief Mark was talking to the news media and that was one less thing Wrenn had to worry about.

Lally and Shawn went into the Cushing house to search for evidence, however, before they did that, they tried to clean the blood on the floor the best they could. After blood leaves the body it will pool and subsequently, begins to coagulate. As it does this, the water separates itself from the blood. As one detective found a mop for the water, the other found a shovel for the then gelatinous blood and put it in a plastic trash bag for disposal.

A more in depth search of the house yielded no clues and they met with Bill Wrenn who was standing next to Tim Collins. It was past midnight.

"Alright we've done everything that we can and the only thing we have for evidence is the screen door which we're taking back to the station. Have we missed anything?" Wrenn said.

"I think we're good," Lally replied.

Tim Collins then chirped in, "Has anyone talked to the neighbors who called it in originally?"

"What are you talking about," Bill Wrenn said.

"Laura and I got the original call that came in from the neighbors to the left, the Smiths. The original report was they thought they heard two shots. It was only after we got here that we learned that Cushing got hit."

"Okay let's do it," Shawn said and he and Bill Lally walked over to the neighbors.

Bill knocked on the door and it was immediately answered.

"Hi Mr. Smith, I'm detective Lally and this is detective Maloney. Sorry to bother you at this hour but as you probably know, Mr. Cushing's been killed and we were informed that you made the original call of shots fired."

"No problem detectives and call me John. Yea I called it in. It sounded really loud and I didn't think it was fireworks, my daughter Linda heard it too. My wife was out shopping at the time."

"Did you see anything?"

"No I didn't, but my daughter was upstairs doing her homework and she may have seen something. Her desk is right by her bedroom window that faces the Cushing house. She's still up."

"Could you get her please?"

"Linda, can you come down here."

Linda was a junior at Winnacunnet High School which was a regional High School for the surrounding towns in addition to Hampton.

"What's up dad?"

"These two detectives would like to know if you saw anything around the Cushing house after we heard the shots earlier tonight."

"Oh yea, I saw two people running down the road coming from Mr. Cushing's house. One was carrying a big stick, and the other had something in his hand, but I didn't know what is was. It looked like a laundry sack."

Which way were they running?" Shawn asked.

"They were running towards the beach."

"Did you notice what they were wearing and can you describe them?"

"Yea, one looked like he had his pajama's on and they were all black. I didn't get a good look at him, but I did the other guy. The other one, the one carrying the stick, had on dark shorts and a light shirt, and he looked younger and smaller with slicked backed light brown hair."

"After they left the house running towards the beach, did you see anything else, maybe a car?"

"No that's it, I only saw them running towards the road and that's all."

"Ok thanks Linda, you've been a big help."

Both detectives walked back to the Cushing house and saw Deputy Wrenn.

"We got something. The daughter, who's in high school, was in her upstairs bedroom doing homework and it faces the Cushing house. She saw two people running from the house towards the beach and gave us a description," Shawn said, and as an afterthought, "they probably had a car parked down the road."

"Well we have something now, two people, probably men and they used a shotgun. This shouldn't be a hard solve, Cushing was obviously targeted and has probably made some enemies along the way. I remember that car accident in '75 when he got arrested, he was somewhat caustic," Wrenn answered.

"Yea I heard about that, we'll have to do a background tomorrow," Bill Lally answered.

"Alright, let's call it a night, and we'll start early tomorrow and get your reports done then," Wrenn answered.

"Gotcha, I'll be in by 7, is that good for you Shawn?" Bill Lally said.

"No problem, I'll see you then."

It was past midnight and the time had gone by quickly. Bill Lally secured the house and a couple of patrol officers took the crime scene tape down. He thought to himself what he had to do in the morning. First on the list was to call Renny Cushing and bring him up to speed, including that they had taken the screen door for evidence. Bill shrugged to himself. That was the only physical evidence they had, and outside of Linda Smith's description of the two possible shooters, that was it.

No one bothered going to Bob and Sammi McLaughlin's apartment to enquire if they had seen or heard anything, since his truck was gone and they thought he was on vacation in Maine.

When Lally got into his car, he tuned the radio to the sports channel. He had all but forgotten about the playoff game. He was disappointed to hear that the Detroit Pistons beat the Celtics by a score of 102-96. It was a bad night all the way around.

****

John Tommasi had just gotten up and was drinking coffee on the farmer's porch at 16 M Street when he saw the headlines in the Eagle Tribune. This was the sixth, and last year that the boys from Salem, PD rented the cottage for the summer on M street. There were only four of them this year and Tommasi was the only who rented it initially in 1983. Fred Rheault was also having coffee with Tommasi.

"Hey Fredso, there was a murder yesterday here in Hampton."

"No shit. They never have murders here."

"Yea, some guy named Cushing who lives uptown."

"Any suspects?"

"Doesn't seem so."

"No shit."

Chapter 2
The Cushing Family

Robert Reynolds Cushing Sr. was born in 1924 In Manchester, NH. His family moved to Hampton and his dad built the house where the family lived. After graduating from Hampton Academy in 1942, he joined the United States Marines and fought in the Pacific theater where he earned a Purple Heart. In 1949, after taking advantage of the GI bill, he graduated from St. Anslem's College. In 1951, he married the love of his life, Marie Cushing, and they settled in Hampton, NH. He taught in various elementary schools and retired from an Amesbury, Ma elementary school after 15 years. After retirement, he worked as a successful real estate agent for the Junkin's and Jackson Century 21 company in Hampton where he won salesman of the year in 1985 and 1987. He was a member and director of the Seacoast Board of Realtors and was involved in the grievance, education and legislative committees. He was 63 at the time of his death.

****

Robert Reynolds Cushing Jr. was born in 1952 and graduated from Winnacunnet High School. He was called Renny (a contraction of his middle name) by family and friends. Renny was the oldest of seven children. He was a political activist from an early age speaking out against the Viet Nam war and was also an antinuclear power activist. He was one of ten people who founded the Clamshell Alliance in 1976. The Alliance had its beginnings in 1975 as the Peoples Energy Project and was directly opposed to Richard Nixon's Project Independence which sought to build 1000 nuclear power plants by 2000. They were relatively successful since only about 125 plants were in operation in 2000.

The Alliance in 1976 took direct aim at the Seabrook Nuclear Power Plant that was under construction in 1976. The power plant was being built by the Public Service Company of New Hampshire and the plan was to build two reactors at the sight in Seabrook, NH, which was just off of route 1. They had helped gather petitions and organize town meeting votes against its construction. In May, 1977, there was a demonstration at the power plant by Alliance members who sought to occupy the grounds of the power plant. They began arriving Friday night and by Sunday, there were over two thousand demonstrators of which fourteen hundred were arrested in a generally peaceful day. The resistance to arrest was passive and most had to be carried aboard the buses that were used to take the prisoners to a National Guard Armory which was used as a temporary jail.

The Alliance was relatively successful. As a result of their actions, the building of the station was extended longer than expected and only one reactor was built instead of two. PSNH was also the first utility in history to declare Chapter 11 bankruptcy. Regardless, the Seabrook Nuclear Plant provides NH residents with 60% of its electricity. Renny was instrumental in relatively everything that happened. Renny's activities came into play significantly during the investigation of his father's murder.

****

Marie Cushing was born, Marie Mulcahey on 4-17-26 in Malden, Ma. She went to Regis College and shortly after graduation, became a social worker at the Fernald School in Waltham, Ma, working with people who had developmental disabilities. She left after several years and became a flight attendant for American Airlines while moving to Hampton, NH in 1950. While in Hampton, she met Robert Cushing and they were married in October of 1951. Marie stopped working while caring for her seven children. Once her youngest entered school in the 1970's, she began teaching at Newmarket Elementary School where she taught reading. Marie later branched out to provide special education services, and took particular pride in her English language instruction to new students.

Katie Wentworth, a new teacher at Newmarket, remembers her as being exceptionally friendly and nurturing, and Marie was respected by all.

Prior to her husband's murder, she was planning on retiring that June and they were planning a trip to Ireland in the fall.

****

There were seven children in the Cushing family and they all shared bedrooms. It was a lifestyle of organized chaos and everyone was close to each other and their parents and that remains to this day.

Chapter 3
The McLaughlin Family

Robert McLaughlin was born Robert Allen Randall on October 10, 1940. He was the youngest of 5 children to his 25 year old mother, Beatrice, who was currently separated from his father, Morris Randall. Beatrice and Morris married in 1932 when she was 17 and two months pregnant. Neither parent had a High School education though Beatrice did complete two years of high school. Morris and Beatrice lived together off and on until Morris went into the service in 1942. By this time, Beatrice wanted a divorce but waited until the end of the war. They were divorced in 1946. Robert remembered stories of beatings that is mother received from the hands of his father from his older siblings and he barely remembered his father. He never witnessed any beatings.

Robert started school in Seabrook, NH, and repeated grade 2. After his mother married his stepfather, U.A. McLaughlin, they moved to Newburyport Ma, just across the state line where Bob attended Kelly School and then Jackman School. Grade 7 was at the Salisbury Memorial School and he was committed while in grade 8. He was described as an average to below average student with an IQ of 91 with no discipline problems. The principle described him as an overall good student and credit to his school.

After the armed robbery in January of 1956, he was committed to Mass juvenile detention center and was paroled in August of 1956 as a result of good behavior and a favorable outcome from counseling. His stepfather subsequently adopted him and that is when Robert changed his last name from Randall to McLaughlin. In 1958, after applying to the US Marines and passing the physical and mental tests at the Haverhill, Ma recruitment center, he was released from probation.

Little is known of McLaughlin's life from 1958 to 1969. It is believed that he did go to marine boot camp but didn't finish for reason(s) unknown. This could in part account for his spit and polish uniform and demeanor later in life.

McLaughlin married in 1962 and had three children, Robert McLaughlin Jr. and two daughters.

In 1969, Robert's cousin, John Campfield, was an officer in the Seabrook, NH Police Department and asked Bob if he wanted to be a part time police officer in Seabrook. At the time, there was no testing to become an officer and any background check was minimal. All that was required was a GED or High School education. Training was done by the Police Department that hired the officer since the Police Standards and Training Counsel wasn't created until 1971 and the first Academy wasn't until 1973, it was 4 weeks long and held at Pease Air Force Base. The recruits slept in barracks and were able to go home on weekends. All existing full-time officers were grandfathered and didn't have to attend.

Authors note: The current academy is 16 weeks long and held at the Police Standards & Training facility in Concord, NH. Recruits are still allowed to return home on weekends. They must pass weekly written test in addition to daily physical requirements, a one week weapons class and a one week defensive driving course..

The background check for McLaughlin in 1970 consisted of a favorable recommendation from his cousin John Campfield, and a local background check. They never knew his original name was Randall or what had happened as a juvenile.

Seabrook and Hampton PD had, and still do, have a very close working relationship, and after McLaughlin found there was a full time opening at Hampton PD, he applied for it and he was offered the job in 1970 which he took. Training in Hampton for full time officers consisted of on the job training by being doubled with a more senior officer, and a 5 day in house class where the officers were exposed to police procedures, tactics, shooting and state criminal laws. Essentially, you were given a badge and you had to buy your own gun and uniform, do a good job with the senior officer and pass a shooting test at the range.

As it turned out, McLaughlin was a quick learner and had an affinity for shooting and police work.

This became evident in his response to the Hampton Falls gun store robbery in October of 1973. In police work, you respond as you were trained. McLaughlin didn't have to think about what he did, it came automatically. He didn't think twice about skipping the shotgun pellets along the hardtop so he would only wound. However, the stress of the situation, particularly the bullets whizzing by his head took its toll. In the early seventies, there was no such thing as an employee assistance program and cops were expected to suck it up. It was part of the job. He really had no one to talk to. His marriage to Beverly, was mediocre at best and she was constantly complaining that he should work more overtime. In the early seventies, the minimum wage was $1.60/hour and as a full-time patrolman, McLaughlin was making only $3.50/hour or $7,280/year.

In 1973, median family income was $12,840 and the poverty level for a family of five was $6500. McLaughlin's pay in 2021 dollars and cents would be $21.70/hour or $45,136/year and the poverty level for a family of 5 is $31,040. Beverly didn't work since she was taking care of 3 young children. The family rented a small house on Lafayette Rd in Seabrook and at times had to resort to food stamps for the children. Needless to say, they lived from paycheck to paycheck. This all contributed to his stress level, and for Robert McLaughlin, stress was cumulative. What also bothered him was that his favorite beer was Lowenbrau, but he couldn't afford it and had to settle for Schlitz or Budweiser.

This stress rose exponentially after he took part in the arrest of Richard Cushing in August of 1975 and Gladys Ring the following month. Cushing not only fought his arrest and tried to get McLaughlin and Mathews fired, but he also pursued them civilly, and for a short period of time attached McLaughlin's bank account which was eventually overturned.

Bob, who was accustomed to having two or three drinks each night after work, increased his alcohol consumption. His marital situation worsened and he and Beverly separated in 1978 and were soon divorced that year. Beverly had custody of their three children. He rented a room from a friend and in order to provide Beverly with child support and living expenses, he began to work overtime which stressed him even more. During this time, he made a half-hearted attempt to commit suicide by taking too many Xanax. He called Rick Mathews who drove him to the Exeter hospital. He was visited by a number of patrolman the next day and was advised to seek help and not report this since it could jeopardize his job. He still couldn't afford Lowenbrau.

In the late seventies to early eighties he applied for a number of positions in the police department such as detective and the newly formed position of School Resource Officer, however he was never picked. He also tested to be promoted to Sergeant. While his score was acceptable, he was never chosen. All these positions would have resulted in more pay.

He blamed Richard Cushing for his lack of advancement because of the Cushing complaints. His resentment for Cushing magnified over the months and years.

McLaughlin was viewed as a good patrolman and was described as a model for the younger recruits since he was always described as being spit and polish with an immaculate uniform and he was a "cop's cop." When he went to pick up his paycheck at town hall, he was described by the clerks as always being respectful and polite, and oftentimes his children accompanied him. He was also described as a model tenant by Margery Castaldy, the building manager for the Elsie St apartments.

During this time, he did become an intoximeter operator and firearms instructor. While the positions resulted in some extra overtime pay, the positions came with no extra money except for the overtime.

Robert McLaughlin lived a very simple life which is evidenced that by the time he turned forty, he had never been out of New England, and his first time on an airplane was when he was flown to a California jail after being convicted of the killing Robert Cushing. He was transported by the Justice Prisoner and Alien Transportation System (JPATS), nicknamed "Con Air".

McLaughlin was very good friends with his two
Sergeants on the day shift, Rick Mathews and John
Campbell. One day during the summer of 1980, Campbell
and McLaughlin had lunch at the Hampton Pizza Hut on
Lafayette road while on duty. They were waited on by the
restaurant manager Susan Cook who was known by Sam or
Sammi to her friends. Sammi explained that she was short-
handed and filling in for one of the girls who called in sick.
She was enamored by Bobby McLaughlin in his uniform.
Bob started coming more frequently and they eventually
started dating. They moved in together within a year and
Sammi and Bob were married shortly thereafter in 1982.
Sammi continued her job as a manager at Pizza Hut and
with her pay, they were able to afford a two bedroom
apartment in an upscale complex. As it happened, their
first floor, corner apartment was right next to the Cushing
residence and McLaughlin was able to look into the
backyard and house at night if the shades were up.

By 1981, child support payments were reduced
since one of the kids reached adulthood, and alimony was
eliminated because Beverly remarried. For the first time
since he was single, Bob McLaughlin was able to afford
Lowenbrau. Not only that, he bought a used motorcycle
and he and Sammi took a trip with it to New York. He had
finally left New England.

****

The stress level for McLaughlin had momentarily
abated. However, since the apartment they were in was
adjacent to the Cushing home, their living room window

gave a direct view to the Cushing back yard. The resentment of Cushing escalated and he had confided in Sammi, who agreed and sympathized with him entirely. By 1984, McLaughlin's stress started to escalate. This stress was evident to his Sergeant, John Campbell. Campbell noticed how withdrawn and moody McLaughlin was becoming and he wasn't getting together with "the guys" at all. Campbell expressed his concerns to Chief Mark in late 1985. He also strongly suggested to Chief Mark that "we get Bob off the streets for a while and pigeon-hole him." Campbell suggested that McLaughlin be assigned to either detectives or as a school resource officer. This never happened and in January, 1986, McLaughlin left on an approved workers comp claim for "psychological difficulties." He began seeing Dr Thomas Lynch of Psychological Associates in Rochester, NH.

Dr Lynch diagnosed McLaughlin as having an extreme panic disorder exacerbated by agoraphobia, a type of anxiety in which you fear and avoid places or situations that might cause you to panic and make you feel trapped. The individual fears an actual or anticipated situation, such as using public transportation, being in open or enclosed spaces, standing in line, or being in a crowd. In McLaughlin's case, he was worried about not knowing what to do in any situation he encountered as a police officer. Lynch found that McLaughlin had these panic attacks going back at least five years and Bob experienced his first attack after the shooting incident of 1973. McLaughlin received little support from his first wife Beverly who told him not to talk to his co-workers about the incident since it might cause him to lose his job. These attacks occurred off and on for a year. When Bob once again mentioned to Beverly that it would help if he could talk to someone at work about it, Beverly told him that his fellow cops would think he's crazy and once again reiterated that it could cost him his job. She seemed more concerned that she would lose means of support as opposed to her husband's mental well-being. After getting separated from Beverly, and then divorced, he did speak to some co-workers which temporarily alleviated some of the attacks. The attacks eventually resumed accompanied by insomnia, possibly because of his lack of advancement in the police department.

Dr Lynch felt that McLaughlin would be able to return to work after 6-8 weeks of counseling where he prescribed Xanax, a medication used to treat panic disorders, and Halcion to help McLaughlin sleep. The weekly sessions constituted a process of systematic desensitization. This is a type of behavioral therapy based on the principle of classical conditioning in which the patient is exposed to progressively more anxiety-provoking stimuli and taught relaxation techniques. Eventually, because of the relaxation techniques, the anxiety-provoking stimuli lose their effect.

McLaughlin never told the doctor about the accidental childhood killing of his best friend.

McLaughlin started his visits the second week of January and unlike Beverly, his second wife Sammi was very supportive, especially in listening to his complaints about Cushing, something McLaughlin didn't tell his therapist.

By the end of January, McLaughlin started taking karate lessons and started jogging. He was getting outside more and began getting together with more friends on social situations. By February, he substituted bike riding for jogging since it wasn't as "rough" on his knees and reported to Dr Lynch that he was sleeping better and was beginning to feel considerably more confident.

The month of February showed even more improvement for McLaughlin. He and his wife continued to go out with friends on a weekly basis and by the second week in February, he went into the station to complete paperwork left over from December. At the end of week three, he worked one shift in uniform in an unmarked cruiser backing up other units. He reported to Dr Lynch that he experienced about two hours of anxiety at the beginning of the shift, but was able to overcome this by employing the relaxation techniques he had learned.

Overall, both McLaughlin and Dr Lynch were pleased with his progress. By the end of the month, they were discussing McLaughlin's return to work.

During the first week in March, McLaughlin reported to Dr Lynch that he had experienced no anxiety during the past week and was ready to return to work full-time which he did the following week. Dr Lynch determined that they would go two weeks before his next appointment. During this session on March 25, McLaughlin reported that he was doing well and was attempting to quit smoking. He was down to under one-half pack per day. He also reported that he had a DWI (Driving While Intoxicated) arrest who was particularly obnoxious and combative and he was happy with his performance and had no anxiety. Unfortunately at this time, his mother was diagnosed with terminal cancer which was a source of sorrow and anxiety for him. Dr Lynch stated that this was normal and he would be concerned if he didn't have those feelings.

They scheduled his next appointment for Thursday, April 10, a little more than two weeks away.

The April 10th meeting was significant. He reported the shootout and high speed chase the previous Saturday, April 5, that involved Joe Galvin, Rick Mathews and the perpetrator, Ken Woodward.

During this meeting, McLaughlin reported that he was doing well since their last meeting, particularly in light of the major shoot out he was involved in the previous weekend. McLaughlin reported that he didn't have any overwhelming anxiety as a result of the incident, however, he felt bad about it the next day since he felt that he could've been killed and didn't want to put that burden on his wife and children. Dr Lynch once again pointed out that this was normal and he would have been more concerned if he didn't have those feelings. McLaughlin also reported that he was rarely taking the Xanax and Halcion that was prescribed for him. Dr Lynch felt that McLaughlin was making good progress and was able to go a month before there next session.

McLaughlin's mother died during the next month and he reported to Dr Lynch that she died in his arms. Of the five siblings, he was the one who provided the main support for his mother and then made all the funeral and burial arrangements. While this was difficult, he was coping.

The last meeting was in June and both McLaughlin and Dr Lynch felt that Bob was doing extremely well. McLaughlin reported that he had been thinking less about his mother's death and also found that he was able to concentrate and function much better on the job. McLaughlin also verified that when he needs to interact with people he stops for a motor vehicle violation, he has no trouble concentrating on the task. He also reported that he is no longer having anxiety attacks, is drinking less and hasn't taken any medication in the past three weeks.

McLaughlin still never told Dr Lynch about his continuing grudge against Richard Cushing who he would murder almost two years to the date.

****

Robert's mother, Beatrice McLaughlin was born in Boston in 1915 and was married to Robert's father, Morris Randall, in 1932 when she was two months pregnant. Over the years, she suffered both mental and physical abuse from Morris and was ready to file for divorce in 1942 when Morris was drafted into the army. She waited until he returned in 1946 to get a divorce and she was granted custody of the children. Robert had little memory of his biological father. In 1948, Beatrice married UA McLaughlin. She was working part-time as a waitress making $26.40/week and was receiving an extra $46.50/month from welfare. A dollar in 1948 was worth about $11 today, so her weekly income in 2021 dollars would be $290 and monthly welfare $511.50. Her marriage to UA McLaughlin was happy and they had no children together. Beatrice described Robert in favorable terms as a trouble-free son and outside of the accidental shooting of Janvrin and the guilt induced armed robbery, she was very proud of Robert. Robert, according to Beatrice, barely remembered his father Morris and lost touch with him completely after Beatrice remarried.

****

UA McLaughlin was born in 1917 in Boston and was a devout Catholic. He had Beatrice convert to Catholicism from Protestant prior to the marriage. This wasn't a problem for the Catholic Church since the Church did not recognize any marriage that wasn't Catholic.

UA McLaughlin only had an eighth grade education and worked as a painter making $70/week, $770 in 2021 dollars. Given both spouses income, they would be classified as middle class at that time. McLaughlin's supervisor described him as being reliable, steady and conscientious. Beatrice described him as a good husband and stepfather to Robert and treated Robert as his own. It appeared the only vice he had was an affinity for alcohol, and he was arrested in 1950 for public drunkenness, however he was on the wagon since that time. After Robert was arrested after the armed robbery, he purged all firearms from the house and remained very supportive of his stepson.

****

Robert's biological father, Morris Randall, was born on 9-26-11 In Seabrook, NH and married Beatrice in 1932. He dropped out of school after his sophomore year and was a chronic alcoholic. Reports indicated that at one time he was committed to the White River Sanitarium in Vermont and while he was drinking, he would disappear for varying lengths of time. He had little to do with the upbringing of the 5 children and Robert's older siblings reported both mental and physically abusive behavior by Morris. At the time of the accidental shooting of Janvrin, he was deceased.

****

Sammi McLaughlin was born Susan Cook in Lewiston, Maine in 1953. She came from a large family, and she was the oldest of four girls and six boys. When she met Bob McLaughlin, she was divorced and had custody of her seven year old, Ray McDaniels Jr. Because of all the hours she was working at Pizza Hut as the manager, one of Sammi's sister and her mother babysat constantly. When she and Bob were engaged, she gave up custody of her son to her first husband. As to why, there is some question. Sammi said that Bob had given her an ultimatum that she had to pick between him or her son. Other's stated that she wasn't much of a mother and had voluntarily given up her son because she wanted to start anew. Either way, after her ex-husband took custody, Sammi had no contact with her son for the next 23 years.

When she was arrested, in September of 1988, she was working at the Old Salt Tavern in Hampton as a cook. She was previously a waitress but sometimes had issues with customers. Her co-workers described her as likable and a good cook. Her manager at the time, Dianne Goode, described her as having a good work ethic but was difficult to get to know, and that she appeared to be under a lot of strain.

Chapter 4
Murder at the Front Door
Wednesday, June 1, 1988

"Sammi can you get me another beer please."

"No problem and I'll join you."

It was Bob McLaughlin's fourth beer of the night and he was beginning to match them one for one with shots of vodka, using the beer as a chaser. Earlier in the evening he had popped a Xanax, the first time in about a week. The anxiety was particularly bad this night, and he was glad he had Sammi.

The TV was on and Apocalypse Now was playing. From his corner apartment next to the Cushing house, he was able to see Marie and Robert watching TV since they hadn't pulled down the shades.

"Look at him, he has an ideal life, and I'm still a patrolman, all because of him. He doesn't deserve to be alive. It's because of him and his liberal son that I was never chosen for Detective or Sergeant."

"Then stop talking about and just do it. You're right, he deserves it," his wife said.

"You're right," McLaughlin said while still sitting at the kitchen table of his two bedroom apartment.

"I've had it, I don't care if I get caught. I'm going to do it. I'm going to do it with my shotgun."

The shotgun was a small sawed off double barrel shotgun with pistol grips that made it easily concealable.

As he got up from the table, he stumbled, but caught himself.

"No wait Bobby," Sammi said. "We need a plan and I'm going with you. I'll drive your truck and be the lookout, but we need a plan and we need to disguise ourselves. We're not going to get caught."

"What do you have in mind Sammi?"

"Go put on your black karate gi, and wear your black pull down hat. I'm going to slick back my hair and wear some clothes that will make me look like a guy. I'll bring your karate staff too. If anyone sees anything, they'll give a description of me and that will throw the investigation off."

Robert was nodding his head. "Okay, let's do it."

While Bob went into the bedroom to change, Sammi went into the bathroom and slicked her long hair back with gel and water. She went into the bedroom and tucked it under a light shirt and then put on purple shots.

"Won't you stick out like that Sammi?"

"That's the idea. This way if anyone sees me, they'll think I'm the killer and give the wrong description to the police. Taking your truck is a good idea. It's dark and it blends in."

"We're not going to just walk over?"

"No, we'll go and park on Presidential Circle, hardly anyone lives there and no one will notice the truck."

Sammi grabbed the karate staff from the closet and Robert took the double barreled sawed-off shotgun from under the bed, and loaded it with solid lead shot."

"This'll punch holes in him the size of baseballs and the shells won't eject. They'll be no evidence," Robert said to Sammi.

After putting the shot gun in a laundry bag they shut off the lights in the house and got into Bob's dark brown Ford truck, Sammi drove.

"Bobby duck down, this way if anyone notices the truck, they'll just see me."

Sammi backed the truck out of the parking space and took a right onto Elsie Street and another right onto Winnacunnet heading east towards the beach. As they drove by the Cushing house they were able to see them through the window. The front door was closed. Bob felt his heart pounding in his chest.

Sammi took a left onto Presidential Drive, made a U-turn and parked about 50 feet from the intersection. Since there were no street lights on Presidential, the truck would be difficult to see from someone driving by on Winnacunnet.

"All right let's go. I'll go first and we'll walk on the sidewalk. It's dark and there are a lot of trees," Sammi said. The sidewalk was on the opposite side of the Cushing residence.

Just before they reached the Cushing house, they saw a slow moving car travelling east on Winnacunnet heading towards the beach.

"Ok Bob, I'm going to cross the street so the people in that car can see me. Wait until it goes by and then you cross."

Robert nodded his head.

As Sammi crossed the road, she was caught in the headlights of the oncoming car.

Mary Cheney was alone in the car and was on her way home from shopping when she saw what she thought to be a thin young man who was carrying a long stick cross the road in front of her. She thought that was strange but didn't think any more of it.

After the car went by, Sammi hid behind a bush on the edge of the Cushing yard and Bob ran across the street. He still had the shotgun in the laundry bag.

"Ok Bobbie, I'll stay here and be a lookout. You do him."

McLaughlin took the shotgun out of the laundry bag and ran across the lawn to the front door of the Cushing house. He was bent down so anyone in the house couldn't see him. He then pounded on the screen door and pointed the shotgun towards the door. He heard someone walking towards the front door. He momentarily wondered what he would do if Cushing's wife answered the door.

"Hold your horses, I'm coming."

It was Robert Cushing's voice. I'm finally going to get even McLaughlin thought.

Cushing opened the door and McLaughlin didn't hesitate. First one barrel and then the other through the screen door. Cushing was propelled backwards over a hallway table. After he shot Cushing, McLaughlin just stood frozen on the porch.

"Run," Sammi shouted.

As McLaughlin was running away he heard a scream from whom he thought was Cushing's wife. When he reached Sammi, they ran across the street and then back to the truck as he put the shotgun back into the laundry sack. His heart was still pounding. They lucked out, and no cars went by them. Sammi got into the driver's seat and took a left out of Presidential onto Winnacunnet heading towards the beach. As she was pulling out from Presidential, she noticed headlights behind her, but they went the opposite direction on Winnacunnet.

Sammi finally spoke, "Did you get him?"

McLaughlin felt himself shaking from the post adrenaline high.

"Yea I got him. Twice in the gut, he's history. We need to get rid of the gun."

"Where, are you going to bury it?"

"No, let's throw it off a bridge. Get onto route 95 and I'll throw it off the Newburyport Bridge going over the Merrimac River. I remember someone telling me once how polluted and silty it is. There's no visibility and it'll sink into the silt. No one will ever find it."

"Alright, but I'll keep my speed down, we don't want to get stopped."

When Sammi got to Ocean Blvd, she took a left.

"Where are you going," Bob asked.

"I'll take a left onto High Street and then pick up 101 to 95. They'll be less people and cars then if we go down by the beach."

"Ok, that's good," Bob answered.

"How do you feel," Sammi said.

"Like a big weight has been lifted from my shoulders."

"Finally, he had it coming," Sammi answered.

A short time later, Sammi pulled over onto the breakdown lane of the Whittier Bridge.

"Alright Bob, there aren't any cars coming."

Bob got out of the car while looking to his left and right, walked to the side of the bridge, took the shotgun out of the bag and threw it into the fast moving waters of the Merrimac where it immediately sank out of sight. He got back into the car.

"We're good now. No evidence can be linked to us," Sammi said.

"Actually there's one more thing. I need to wash my clothes as soon as we get back."

"What do you mean," Sammi asked.

"Gunshot residue. Whenever you fire a gun, you can't see it, but residue blows back onto your clothes and hands. I'll need to take a shower too."

"Good thinking Bob. I'll throw away these purple shorts. I'm working tomorrow and I'll throw them in the dumpster at the Old Salt. That car that drove by saw me in those shorts. So now, they'll really be no evidence.

When Sammi drove back, they got off on route 1 from 101 and entered Winnacunnet from the West side. When they got back to their apartment complex, they were able to see the cruisers and police tape around the Cushing residence.

"I'll let you off in the front Bob, this way no one will see you."

"How 'bout you Sam?"

"There's an open parking space up front, and then I'll come in through the front door too."

When Sammi came into the house the washing machine was going and Bob was in the shower.

Sammi changed her clothes, threw the purple shorts in a trash bag and took them out to her car.

By this time, everyone had cleared the scene from the Cushing house. When Sammi came back into the apartment, Bob was out of the shower and having a vodka with another beer chaser and was making a phone call. He was calling the police station.

"Hi, it's Bobby Mac. What's going on next door at the Cushing house? Sammi and I just got home from a night out."

"Not going to believe this but someone killed Cushing. Two shotgun slugs to the gut. Never had a chance."

"Any suspects or evidence?"

"Not a thing."

Alright then, I'll see you tomorrow.

"That was the station, they got nothing," McLaughlin said to Sammi.

"Good, let's have a drink and then go to bed."

"Sounds good."

****

The next morning McLaughlin arrived at work with his usually spit and polish appearance and didn't participate in the banter about the previous night's murder.

Linda Coventry was in work early at the Old Salt and noticed that Sammi McLaughlin was in early too. She was throwing something in the dumpster and Linda thought that was odd, Sammi's never in this early. She didn't think any more of it.

Chapter 5
The Investigation, June

At 6:30 AM, June 2, Bill Lally was at his desk in detectives. He noticed that the local TV stations were set up in front of and on the side of the police station. He had a coffee from Dunkin Donuts that he picked up on the way to work and turned the TV on to channel 9, WMUR. It wasn't long before an on the scene reporter started talking about the murder.

"There is little to go on Jack. What we do know is that Robert Cushing Sr., a well-respected resident of Hampton, was killed sometime last night. Sources tell us, a shotgun was used. Outside of that, police are being tight-lipped and we have little information other than that."

Shawn Maloney and Bill Wrenn were in by seven and they began evaluating what they had, which wasn't much. Shortly after seven, Chief Bill Wrenn, Sergeant Mike Simmons, Bill Lally and Sean Maloney were in their first of many meetings concerning the Cushing murder.

Chief Wrenn started the meeting. "You guys will be working this case full time and I'll give you whatever support you need. We'll have daily meetings every morning and a wrap up at night. Whatever overtime you need, you take. Just give me a heads up."

After a pause, Wrenn continued. "There's no doubt in my mind, this wasn't random and Cushing was targeted. Let's do this by the numbers. Mike why don't you head to the hospital for the autopsy. You've been to one of those before haven't you?"

"Yea, I have my vics vapor rub with me and a mask. They never get easy."

"I know, but that's why you make the big bucks," Wrenn said kiddingly.

"Thanks."

He turned to Lally, "Bill why don't you start with the family. Get everyone's address and numbers from Renny. See if there were any domestic issues. If I'm not mistaken, it's a big family and it's not uncommon for a family member to be the guilty person."

"Yea," Lally answered. "I and some of the other guys have been at the house on loud party calls and the first thing they say is "Where's your search warrant?" We've never made any arrests but it wasn't friendly."

Shawn Maloney, then spoke up, "It's been like that since the old man was arrested in front of his house after that double fatal accident."

"Yea, I was there," Wrenn answered.

"He wouldn't put out his cigarette with leaking gas on the ground, and he walked right in front of Kennedy who was taking pictures. That was when we arrested him. And then, the very next month he tried to get Mathews and McLaughlin fired after they arrested his neighbor."

"No shit?" Lally said. Then kiddingly with a laugh, "Maybe we should be looking at one of those two."

"Everyone's a comedian," Wrenn answered.

"Okay, back on target, Shawn, you head to Amesbury PD and talk to someone in dicks and see if Cushing had any issues when he was teaching school there."

"No problem, I've got a couple of contacts there."

"Sounds good, anything else," Wrenn asked.

"Nothing? Ok, let's do it and we'll meet back here at four. In the meantime, Chief Mark is giving me the job of talking to the press."

"Lucky you," Simmons said.

****

Bill Wrenn was answering a few of the reporter's questions. He had worn his best suit in anticipation of going before the TV cameras.

"We have little to say outside that we can confirm that it was Robert Cushing Sr. who was murdered last night at approximately 8:30 PM, and any further questions should be directed to Barbara Keshen at the Attorney General's office who will be coordinating the investigation. However, if there was anyone in that area who saw or heard anything, anything at all, no matter how inconsequential you think it may be, or if you have any information, please call the police station."

****

Bill Lally started by first calling Renny Cushing. After enquiring as to how he and his mother were doing, he asked for his sibling's addresses and phone numbers.

"Why do you want that?" Renny asked.

"I need to talk to everyone as to where they were and find out if anyone, including you, know of anyone who may have a grudge against your dad. In addition, I need to take fingerprints from everyone to eliminate them."

"I resent any implication about my family and what do you mean to eliminate them."

Bill Lally was being his best understanding self, even though Renny was beginning to push some buttons.

"I realize that Renny, and I doubt any of your family was involved, but this is required by the assistant AG Barbara Keshen and our investigation needs to be one-hundred percent complete. We were able to get some prints from the front screen door. It was a smooth varnished surface. If none of the prints on the door match you or your siblings, there's a chance they could belong to the murderer. No you don't have to give names and addresses to me, but I could find out where they live through the motor vehicle department and visit them with a marked cruiser and a court order to get their prints, but I would prefer not to do that."

After a pause, "Alright, give me a minute while I get my address book and my prints should already be on file from my arrest when I was one of fourteen hundred demonstrators arrested at the Seabrook nuke in the seventies."

"Thanks, much appreciated and I'll check for your prints."

****

It took all day, but Bill was able to contact the other six siblings: Mathew, Kevin, Timothy, Michael, Christine and Mayrnia. To no surprise, most took umbrage over having to produce an alibi, but once they were past that, everyone was generally cooperative. If it's one thing he learned, the Cushing family was a loving family and no suspicions were raised as to whether they may have committed the murder. None had any idea who may have had any kind of grudge towards their father and their father was not involved in anything that they were aware which would have created animosity against him. Bill set appointments for the siblings to come into the station over the next 3 days for elimination prints. A few did mention their father's arrest in 1975 and spoke poorly of the Hampton Police Department, but no one suggested that an officer may have done the shooting.

****

Before going to the Amesbury Elementary school where Robert Cushing had taught for 15 years, Shawn Maloney went to the real estate company where Cushing worked for the past 3 years, Junkin's and Jackson Century 21, in Hampton, at 836 Lafayette rd.

After introducing himself, Shawn asked about Robert Cushing. Both Junkin's and Jackson had nothing but good things to say about him. He was personable, and his clients liked, and more importantly, trusted him; that's why he won the realtor of the year award in 1985 and 87.

"Do you know anyone who didn't like him or may have a grudge against him," Maloney asked.

Both partners looked at each other and shook their heads.

"Not a person," Lloyd Jackson answered.

He went on, "I don't even remember any complaints. Conversely, Cushing never said a bad word about anyone."

"Okay thanks. If you should remember anything, anything at all, let me know and he's my card," Shawn said.

"No problem and we'll be happy too."

****

It was the same thing at the Cashman elementary school in Amesbury. Shawn learned that Cushing taught there from 1975-1982 before going on to the junior high school from 1982 to Spring of 84, at which time he retired, obtained his real estate license, and went to work for Junkin's and Jackson.

At both schools, he spoke to everyone in Cushing's department, plus the secretaries and principles. All spoke in nothing but superlatives concerning Cushing and no one had anything negative to say. Shawn realized that this was usually the case when someone was deceased, especially by murder. On the way to his car he saw a telephone booth and called into the station.

"Hampton Police, may I help you, dispatcher Ganley."

"Hi Mary Jo, it's Shawn, is Chief Wrenn in?"

"Yes he is, I'll put you through to him."

"Deputy Chief Wrenn, can I help you."

"Hi Chief it's Shawn."

"How'd it go today?" Wrenn asked.

"Didn't get a thing, everyone put this guy on a pedestal and no leads as to who may have disliked him, let alone wanted him dead."

"Okay, come on in and check with Lally and Simmons, then we'll meet at four.

"Got ya."

****

Mike Simmons had been to autopsies before and while he had the stomach and attitude for it, there were more pleasant aspects of the job. Simmons was in the cellar of Concord hospital and waiting for the Chief Medical Examiner, Roger Fossum outside of the autopsy room. The autopsy was scheduled for 11:30 AM.

After being declared dead at Exeter hospital, Cushing's body was transported to Concord where autopsies are performed. Two big differences from a regular operating room is the lower temperature to preserve the body and it was not a completely sterile atmosphere since infection of the deceased was no longer an issue.

In a couple of minutes, Mike saw the elevator doors open and Dr Fossum walked down the corridor with his assistant.

"Hi Doc, how you doing?"

"Good Mike, meet my new assistant, Devin Gillis, he's doing his residency at the hospital and is looking at a career in forensic medicine."

Simmons extended his hand, "Good to meet you."

"You too sir."

"Call me Mike, my dad's sir," Simmons said with a smirk.

"Will do," Gillis said laughing.

"Have you done one of these before?"

"I have, this will be my third."

Mike nodded his head and thought to himself that was good, he wouldn't have to worry about him getting sick, even if he was an intern.

"Alright, let's get to work then," Fossum said.

As they walked into the autopsy room, Mike dabbed some vicks vapor rub into his nostrils and put on his facemask. He noticed that neither Fossum nor Gillis used vicks, but they did wear masks.

As they reached the table, Fossum turned on his new cassette tape recorder and began to describe the deceased.

"Subject is a 63 year old male, five foot ten inches, 190 pounds. He has been positively identified as Robert Cushing of Hampton, NH. A prior toxicology report showed no toxins in the subject's body and a blood alcohol content of .04, which is consistent with two alcoholic beverages in a two to three hour period for a male subject of this size and weight. There were no positives for any other types of drugs The cause of death appears to be massive internal hemorrhaging as a result of what appears to be two shotguns wounds."

After a brief pause where Fossum and Gillis traded places, Fossum continue.

"Intern Devin Gillis will make the torso incision under my tutelage."

Simmons new that it was typical to have an experienced intern do this, especially with a cause of death that was obvious.

Gillis began to make the Y shaped incision of the torso and began to remove the organs and weigh them. Simmons noticed that Gillis had steady hands and he was not fazed by the goriness of the damage done by the shotgun slugs. As Gillis performed the autopsy, Fossum continued to narrate.

"Mike, I take it that you'll need the shotgun slugs for evidence?" Gillis said.

"Yea, shotguns are usually sold with two barrels, a smooth barrel for birdshot and other multiple rounds, and a grooved barrel for slugs. Gives it more accuracy and a little more distance."

"Thanks, I'm feeling one now."

Gillis then got a rubber tipped forceps and removed the shotgun slug and placed it in a metal tray. Simmons looked at Fossum and he nodded. Simmons then retrieved the slug, washed it out with water from a bottle that was present and bagged and tagged the slug as evidence. The reason that Fossum didn't do this was because it would be one less person in the chain of custody.

The same procedure was mirrored when the second shotgun shell was located. Simmons noticed that there were very distinct rifling marks on both slugs. The gunshot wounds were noted to be in the upper right chest which punctured a lung, and the abdomen slightly to the left.

After Gillis completed the autopsy, he put the organs in plastic bags to prevent leakage, replaced them in the chest and abdomen cavity and sewed Cushing up.

Fossum noted that the cause of death was massive internal blood loss and shock, and there would be no need for a brain autopsy.

Fossum then turned to Mike after he shut off the recorder, Mike this guy was dead within a minute, probably instantaneously from shock if that's any consolation to the family.

"Thanks Doc, I'll let them know."

Simmons then turned towards Gillis, "Nice meeting you and good job today."

"Thanks, I have a good teacher."

With that, everyone said their goodbyes and Mike headed back to Hampton. On the way he realized he didn't have lunch and despite the blood and guts morning, he stopped at a sub shop on the way back and ordered a meatball sub.

****

No sooner had Bill Wrenn gotten back to his office after his early morning meeting with his detectives and then talking to the media, he received a call.

"Deputy Chief Wrenn, may I help you."

"Hello Chief, this is assistant AG Keshen."

"Hi Barbara, and call me Bill. What can I do for you?"

"I called for an update."

"Well there's little to update you on from last night. Bill is contacting the Cushing children, Sergeant Simmons is on his way to Concord for the autopsy, and Shawn is talking to his employers at the real estate office and the Amesbury schools where Cushing taught. He's also going to Amesbury PD to see if they have any info."

"Will they be working through the weekend?" Keshen asked.

"Yes they will. I told them overtime is not an issue and we'll be exploring every avenue."

"Alright Chief, call me if you find everything."

"You'll be the first to know Barbara."

As he hung up, Wrenn was hoping she wouldn't be a pain. He would be disappointed.

****

At 4 PM, the three detectives and Chief Wrenn were in his conference room.

"Alright everyone, what do we have?" Wrenn asked.

Everyone related the events of the day.

"Yea chief, you should know that Renny and his other siblings were very unhappy about having to come in for fingerprints. They felt that we were accusing them," Lally said.

"I'm not surprised, but again, it's not uncommon for someone in the family to do the killing. We have to do it and eliminate them as suspects."

"It should be a fun weekend interviewing them," Lally answered and then continued, "I know, that's why I make the big bucks."

"Took the words out of my mouth."

"Chief we should probably start canvassing the neighborhood to see if anyone saw anything," Simmons said.

"Good idea Mike, you and Shawn do that tomorrow. Check that apartment building that Bob McLaughlin lives in too. There's several apartments that face the Cushing home. Okay, anything else people?" Wrenn asked.

"Alright then, tomorrow at seven."

****

Renny Cushing spent the day with his mom after talking with detective Lally and calling a remediation company to clean the hallway and living room of his mother's house. There was still some residual blood and fingerprint powder. Marie was going to spend another night at Renny's before going back home, and Renny, his brother Kevin and his sister Christine were going to stay with her in the short term.

After talking with Bill Lally, Renny was extremely upset that there would even be an insinuation that either he or one of his siblings were under suspicion. He had no faith in the Hampton Police Department, particularly after they had previously arrested his dad and neighbor, Gladys Ring. The more he thought about it the more he was upset and then decided to call Barbara Keshen.

****

Barbara hung up with Renny Cushing and decided to go see the Attorney General, Steve Merrill.

Steve had been part of a Manchester law firm and was former Governor John Sununu's personal attorney before he was appointed New Hampshire's chief law enforcement officer by Governor Sununu. Prior to that, he had enlisted in the Air Force after receiving his law degree, and served from 1972 to 1976.

One of his keystone achievements was the establishment of the NH Drug Task Force which was comprised of State Troopers and officers from local departments that were loaned to the task force. It was his springboard to the NH governorship in 1992. He was a former resident of Hampton, and a graduate of Winnacunnet High School before going on to the University of New Hampshire and then Georgetown Law. He was an acquaintance of some of the Cushing siblings. He was also a staunch republican and had views the polar opposite of Renny Cushing, a liberal democrat and state representative from Hampton. He didn't know it, but he was also the polar opposite of Barbara Keshen, who sympathized with Renny's views.

Steve's door was open when Keshen knocked.

"Hi Steve, can I talk to you. It's important."

"Sure come on in and what's up."

"I'll be succinct. I got a call from a very upset Renny Cushing who's complaining about the Hampton Police. It seems that they insinuated that he and his siblings are suspects and they have to come in for fingerprints. I understand why they have to come in but he didn't like the officer's attitude. He wants State Police to do the investigation."

"Barbara, are you aware of the relationship the Cushing's have with Hampton Police."

"I've heard rumors."

"The victim, Robert Cushing Sr. was arrested by them in the mid 70's, something about interfering with an accident scene, and the same year, both Robert Cushing and Renny tried to get a couple of the cops fired for arresting a neighbor. It went nowhere. Add to that the police have been called to their house a number of times for loud parties, and there's no love lost."

After Barbara took this in, she made a mental note to ask both Renny and Bill Wrenn about it and said, "Any chance you think we can convince Hampton to allow state police to take this over?"

"Barbara, I know both Bob Mark and Bill Wrenn, there's no chance, but let me think about it."

"Okay, thanks Steve, I'll touch base with you tomorrow."

****

Mary Cheney had a long day at work when she came home and turned on the local news. What she heard stopped her in her tracks. She couldn't believe that there had been a murder down the street from her. Robert Cushing had been killed and the police were looking for any potential witnesses. She remembered that she had gone by the Cushing home at around the time of the murder when she was coming back from shopping. She also remembered seeing a young man walk across the street with a stick. Did this have anything to do with the murder? She heard Deputy Chief Wrenn on TV ask for any help from the public if they had seen or heard anything. After a few more minutes of debating, she called the station.

****

"Hampton Police, Dispatcher Ruonala."

"Hi, my name is Mary Cheney and I live on Winnacunnet road by the Cushing's."

"Yes ma'am."

"Well, when I was coming home last night, it was around the time the news said the murder happened, and I saw a young man cross the road right by the Cushing House."

"Okay ma'am, let me get your information and I'll contact Detective Lally who's on call tonight. He should be in touch with you shortly if that's convenient?"

"It is."

After getting Mary's information, Ruonala looked up Bill Lally's phone number.

"Hi Bill, it's Fred."

"Hey Fred, what's up"

"I just got a call from a neighbor of Cushing's. She said she was driving home from shopping that night right around the time that Cushing was murdered and she saw someone cross the street right by the Cushing House. She got a description too and I have her info and phone number."

"Outstanding."

After Bill wrote down Mary Cheney's phone number and information, he hung up.

"What was that? You sounded exited," his wife Sandy asked.

"That was the station. We might have a potential witness."

"That's good."

Bill then grabbed his gun and jacket and headed into the station. He was going to call Mary Cheney from there.

****

"Hello."

"Hello, Mrs. Cheney this is detective Bill Lally from Hampton PD, you called the station earlier."

Mary had caller id on her phone and she was able to confirm that the phone number was from the Hampton Police Department.

"Hi Detective Lally, and please, call me Mary."

"Absolutely, and thank you for calling the station. Mary, can you tell me what you saw last night please?"

"Yes. I was coming home from shopping and driving home."

"Were you driving east towards the beach on Winnacunnet?" Lally asked.

"Yes I was. It was dusk and I had my lights on when I saw this person cross the street. I didn't get a good look, but I think it was a young man in his early twenties."

"When you saw this person, had you already passed the Cushing house?"

After thinking about it she answered, "Yes I did, just. I was about twenty feet passed it. I remember that I had to hit my brakes fairly quickly."

"Which way was this person crossing?"

"He, I think it was a he, was walking from my left to my right."

"So he was walking south."

"Yes he was."

"Can you describe him and what he was wearing?"

"He was small and average to thin."

"About how tall and think of yourself for comparison purposes."

"I'd say he was taller than five and half feet but nowhere near six feet. I didn't get a very good look."

"Alright that's fine. Did you see what he was wearing?"

"Yes, I remember that he was wearing lavender shorts and a light colored shirt. Maybe white or yellow and I think sneakers."

"That's good, how about his face.

"He had slicked back hair, like it was jelled. It wasn't dark but it was either light brown or dirty blonde."

"How about his face. Did you notice any facial hair or distinguishing Mark?"

"I'm sorry, I didn't see his face at all."

"How about his complexion?

"He was white, and I don't think much of a tan."

"Thanks Mary, this is very helpful. Let me go over everything to make sure I have it right.

After Bill recapped everything, Mary said, "That's correct"

"Again, thank you very much Mary. Would you be able to come into the station sometime and make a written statement?"

"Sure. Is tomorrow okay after work, about 5 o'clock."

"That would be fine and I'll try to be at the station. Now think for a minute. Is there anything else?"

"Actually yes. When I was bringing in the groceries, I heard two bangs. I thought they were fireworks but now I guess they were shots."

"Quite possibly and thanks again."

After hanging up, Bill typed a notice with the intent of putting it out to the patrol units and walked over to dispatch.

"Hi Fred, we got some info about someone in the area at the time of the murder. Looks a little suspicious." He then handed copies of the description Mary Cheney gave him.

"Huh, wearing lavender shorts," Fred said to no one in particular.

"Yea, that jumped out at me too. Not many guys wear lavender shorts."

"Yea that is unusual, but it takes all kinds. By the way, I ran a record check or Mary Cheney, outside of a warning for speed, we got nothing on her."

"That's good. She seemed reliable. I'll be in my office for about an hour. I'm going to write this up and give Wrenn a call. If anything else comes in, put it through," Bill said as he turned to leave dispatch.

"No problem."

****

"Hi Chief, it's Lally."

"Hi Bill, what's up?"

"We may have something." Bill then brought the Deputy Chief up to speed on the information he received from Mary Cheney.

"Well that's something. I'm hoping to have this solved soon."

"Me too. See you in the morning.

Both Bill Lally and Bill Wrenn knew that if a murder wasn't solved in the first several weeks, the odds of it being solved declined rapidly.

****

The following morning at 7 AM, Bill Lally brought Shawn Maloney and Sergeant Simmons up to date on the information from Mary Cheney.

"A young man, I wonder if that's an ex-student of Cushing's who had a grudge?"

"Possible," Lally said. "But what struck me as odd was a guy wearing lavender shorts. You generally don't see that and Mary Cheney wasn't one hundred percent sure that it was a man, and her description doesn't contradict the neighbors, Linda Smith"

"That's something we'll keep in mind when we canvas the neighborhood today," Maloney said.

"Alright, catch up on paperwork then we'll hit the bricks," Wrenn said. "Bill, you have some of the siblings coming in today?"

"I do and then Mary Cheney said she'll be coming in after work."

"Okay see you guys at the end of the day again."

As Bill Wrenn walked back to his office, he had to walk by dispatch,

"Hey Chief, Barbara Keshen is on line one for you."

Wonderful, Wrenn thought to himself. As he went into his office he picked up his phone.

"Hello Barbara, what can I do for you?"

"Just want to know where we are."

"Well, Simmons and Maloney are canvassing the area ringing doorbells to see if anyone saw anything and we may have a description of the shooter or possibly an accomplice."

"What do you mean?" Keshen asked.

"A woman who lives in the neighborhood saw what she believed to be a young man cross the road towards the Cushing house just before he was shot. She was bringing in the groceries when she heard the shots that she originally thought were fireworks."

"That's good. Your men should keep a lookout for him as they go door to door."

"Thank you Barbara," Wrenn said with a hint of sarcasm.

"But we know what to do."

"Just trying to help and be thorough Chief," Keshen answered somewhat miffed.

"Of course, if there's nothing else, I'll be getting to work."

As Keshen hung up, she purposely didn't tell him about Renny Cushing's phone call.

****

Billy Donovan was a special officer in Hampton who lived down the street from the Campbell's on Presidential Circle. Like everyone else, he was stunned about the Cushing murder. He was on his lunch break from his full time job when he received a call from his brother Rick.

"Hey Bill, how you doing?"

"Good, what's up Rick?"

"You know when I was over your house the other night. That was the night your neighbor was shot, what's his name, Cushing?"

"Yea that's it, Robert Cushing. And those booms we heard as you were leaving that we thought were fireworks, those were the actual gun shots."

"Wow, well I heard on the news that if we heard or saw anything, we should call."

"Yea. Did you see anything?"

"I think so. As I turned onto Winnacunnet heading west, I saw this car peal out and it was heading west towards the town center. There were two people in the car."

"What kind of car?"

"It was a dark colored Mercury Marquis."

"Are you sure."

"Yea, that's the same car as my wife's. I'm pretty positive."

"How about a registration or color plate?"

"I didn't get the registration but I remember the plate was green on white, so probably New Hampshire, and I'm pretty sure there were two people in the car. Both in the front seat."

"Any description?"

"I think they were young."

"Are you home now?"

"Yea I took a long weekend."

"Okay, stay there. I'm going to call the station and tell them and you should get a call from one of the detectives."

"No prob, I'll be home for a few hours."

"Talk to you later."

Bill then called the station and he was put through to Bill Lally who was in his office after fingerprinting and establishing an alibi for one of the Cushing siblings. Like Renny, the first sibling he spoke to was somewhat upset about being treated like a suspect. Bill tried to explain how it was procedure but it fell on what he thought was deaf ears.

"Billy what's up?" Lally answered.

"I may have some information for you Lall."

"Good we could use it."

"I just got a call from my brother who was over my house the night Cushing was killed. He left about the same time Cushing was murdered because we heard the shots."

Donovan then relayed to Lally what his brother told him and gave him his brother's phone number.

After Lally called Rick Donovan and got his story, he went in to see Bill Wrenn.

"Hey Chief, we may have something else."

"Great, what do you have?"

Bill then told the Chief about Rick Donovan's story to his brother.

"Follow me to dispatch," Wrenn said while getting up from his desk. Mary Jo Ganley was on the desk.

"MJ, can you contact state police and get a listing of all Mercury Marquis' in Rockingham county."

"I can do that."

"How long do you think it will take?" Wrenn asked.

"We should have it by this afternoon."

"Excellent, give it to detective Lally when you're done."

"Understood."

"MJ, I'll be in my office all day."

"Yes sir."

Mary Jo was a competent and experienced dispatcher who was well liked by all. Her dad, John Ganley, was the Chief of Police in Salem, NH.

"Just thought of something MJ, once you get the listings, can you run the registered owner, I'm looking to see if any of them have a slight build to match our description of someone leaving the scene."

"Good thinking Bill," Wrenn said.

"Chief if this runs past the end of my shift, I can finish this after it."

"Thanks MJ and put in for the overtime," Wrenn said.

"I'm going to let Chief Mark know," Wrenn said to Lally as they were walking out of dispatch.

****

As Bill Wrenn walked into Chief Mark's office, he hesitated when he saw him on the phone. Bob waved him in and pointed to the door. Bill closed it behind him.

"Alright Steve, I'll see you Monday."

"That was Steve Merrill, he's coming Monday to talk to Renny Cushing," Mark said.

"Why's he doing that?"

"It appears that Renny called Barbara Keshen and he doesn't want us to do the investigation and that he's upset over his siblings having to be fingerprinted and having to establish an alibi."

"That's too bad, Renny's always been anti-police and knows nothing about police procedure."

"You're preaching to the choir Bill. But he's a prominent representative in the Democratic Party and Merrill wants to make nice. Word is Steve's thinking about running for governor at some point in the future."

Wrenn just nodded his head.

"On another note Bob, we may have something."

"What is it?"

"Well in addition to a witnesses' description of the possible shooter, we may have a description of the getaway vehicle."

"Really?"

"Yea, one of our part time officers, Bill Donovan, lives on Presidential Circle and his brother was over visiting. When he was leaving, they heard the shots, which they thought were fireworks, and saw two people leaving in a dark colored Mercury Marquis. He was positive it was a Marquis because his wife has one. Mary Jo is getting listings of all Marquis' in Rockingham County and then running the owners."

"That's excellent. It would be something if we could have this wrapped up by Monday," Mark said.

"Possible, we're all working this weekend."

"Good, I'll be around too."

No one knew that the Marquis was a wild goose chase and the people in the Marquis were just leaving the neighborhood.

****

That afternoon at 5 PM, Mark joined Wrenn, Lally, Simmons and Maloney in Detectives. Bob Mark started the meeting by bringing them up to date on Steve Merrill's visit on Monday. Groans followed Chief Mark' news.

"Shawn and Mike, how'd you guys make out today?" Wrenn asked.

"Nothing new. Some of the neighbors heard the shots and like everyone else, they thought they were either fireworks or a car backfiring," Simmons answered.

"Lall you're next," Wrenn said.

Bill told then about Bill Donovan's brother and the Mercury Marquis.

"Mary Jo had state police give us a listing of all Mercury Marquis' in Rockingham County. There are thirty eight and about twenty are dark colored. There are a few registered owners that match the possible shooters description."

"Good," Simmons said.

"Why don't we do this," Wrenn said and continued.

"Can everyone make it in tomorrow?"

After seeing everyone nod, he went on.

"Okay, let's meet at 9 AM tomorrow and we'll hit the list of registered owners."

Everyone nodded again.

"See you then."

On the way out, Chief Wrenn made it a point to drop by dispatch and see Mary Jo.

"Nice job MJ and thanks"

"Anytime chief," Mary Jo said smiling.

****

It was a frustrating weekend for Hampton's detectives which was evident at the 7 AM Monday meeting.

Bill Wrenn started the meeting attended by Lally, Simmons and Maloney. Between the four of them they put in full days on Saturday and Sunday.

"It looks like we got nowhere with the Marquis. They either didn't match the description and pretty much everyone had an alibi."

"Maybe if we expand the search state wide," Simmons said.

"Possibly," Wrenn said and went on.

"Any other suggestions?"

"I got the elimination prints and alibis of all the siblings," Lally said.

"And as you can probably guess, none of them are happy they had to give prints or supply alibis, but I'm almost positive the siblings had nothing to do with the murder. When they weren't mad at me, they were all pretty broken up."

"Let's do this. Go to dispatch Lall and get a listing of Marquis' from surrounding counties, Strafford, Merrimack and Hillsborough. Shawn, head back to Amesbury and see if anyone you spoke to has remembered anything new since last week. Also, stop in at Newbury and Salisbury PD's, maybe there was some interaction there."

"Mike you catch the tough one and it's a long shot. The wake for Cushing is this afternoon from twelve to four at Remicks. It'll also double as a funeral service. Take the camera and sit across the street. Get shots of everyone going into the funeral home in the off chance the killer attends the funeral."

"Yea I know, that's why I make the big bucks."

"Absolutely."

This was good police work on the part of Bill Wrenn. It was a well-known fact that arsonists will generally always be part of the crowd watching the fire they set. It is also possible that killers want to see the results of their work. It was also a given fact that some killers like to take mementos of their victims.

Little did the detectives and Chief Wrenn know, the killer would be displayed prominently on some of their pictures.

****

Before Deputy Chief Wrenn went to his office, he went to the roll call room and brought the day Sergeant, John Campbell, up to speed on the investigation and the wake and funeral.

"John, can you assign a patrolman to do traffic in front of Remicks at noontime for the Cushing wake and funeral."

"No problem Chief, I've got two extra cops today working the beach and I'll rotate them out every hour."

Bob McLaughlin was at roll call taking this in. His stress level over the weekend was over the top and the last thing he wanted to do was be near any of the Cushing's, let alone be at the wake.

"Bob," Sergeant Campbell said.

"Yea sarge,"

"You're looking good as usual, why don't you take the first hour.

"No problem sarge."

No one noticed his slight hesitation before answering or could they tell the stress he put himself under.

****

When Bill Wrenn went back to his office, it took 5 minutes before he received a call from Barbara Keshen.

"Hello Barbara," he said trying to keep his voice normal and then brought her up to date on the events of the weekend.

"I wished you would have called me Friday with that info."

"Why Barbara? Nothing panned out and it would have been a waste of time."

"I could've helped."

"Thank you but we know how to do our job."

There was a pause at the other end and Barbara then changed tack.

"I'll probably see you later on today. Steve and I will be dropping by the Cushing's later this morning. The wake and funeral is in the afternoon."

"I know we have a guy there taking pictures of people going to the funeral in the off chance the killer is there."

"Do you think that's a good idea?"

"Yes Barbara I do."

There was another pause.

"Goodbye Bill, we'll talk later."
Wrenn reserved comment and also hung up.

****

Renny Cushing was with his mother at her home with his brother Kevin and his sister Christine.

Barbara Keshen knocked on the front door accompanied by Steve Merrill. Renny answered the door and Barbara introduced Steve Merrill to him. Even though neither of them had met before, they recognized each other. Barbara and Renny were developing a mutual respect for each other. They both shared very liberal viewpoints in addition to being jaundiced towards the police. Renny then introduced Steve and Barbara to his siblings. They all sat in the living room after coffee was offered and refused.

"I can't begin to tell you how sorry I am for your loss," Steve Said.

"Thank you," was all Marie said.

"I'm here to tell you that you will have the full cooperation of my office and the Hampton Police Department, and I'm here to assure you, that we have the utmost confidence in the police department."

Keshen said nothing.

"I'm glad you do Steve. We certainly don't, and we would prefer the state police doing the investigation," Renny answered.

"I'm aware of the history your family has with the Hampton Police, but I'm aware of the officers conducting the investigation and they're reporting directly to Deputy Chief Wrenn who is extremely competent. They had three officers, plus Chief Wrenn working the entire weekend and progress is being made."

"We'd still be happier with state police."

"I understand, but I believe you know the law. In NH, if there's a murder in any community with more than three thousand people, it's the Police Chief's choice as to whether his department or State Police conduct the investigation. Both Chief Mark and Deputy Chief Wrenn were adamant that they would do it. We are giving them all the support they want and need, but it's their investigation and I want to express to you that Barbara and I trust Hampton PD's procedure and competence."

"Well thank you for showing up Steve and Barbara, my family and I are grateful and we'll be in touch."

"Once again, my condolences."

As Steve and Barbara entered his car, Steve turned to Barbara.

"Well what do you think?"

"It was a nice gesture, but I don't think Renny or the family is satisfied. And I also wonder if Hampton is in over their head in this investigation."

"I don't think they are Barbara, from what you told me they're doing everything right. Let's head to the PD and see what's going on."

Keshen just nodded.

****

It was eleven-thirty AM when Steve Merrill and Barbara Keshen walked in the front door of the PD. They were recognized by the on duty dispatcher and were buzzed in through the security door. Sergeant John Campbell was in the supervisor's office and walked out to meet them. He shook both their hands.

"Hi Steve, Hi Barbara, I take it your here to see the Chief."

"Yes we are."

"Okay, follow me."

"Chief Mark had already been notified by dispatch and was on his way out of his office to meet them when Campbell arrived at his office door."

"Hi Steve, glad to see you. Hi Barbara. Please come in and have a seat. John can you get Bill Wrenn and ask him to join us?"

"Right away chief."

Bill entered the office, exchanged pleasantries and sat down. He had closed the door on his way in.

Merrill wasted no time, "We just came from the Cushing house and they would like state to do the investigation."

"I'm not surprised," Mark answered.

"But that's not happening," Mark continued.

"That's what I told him and as you can guess that's not the answer he was looking for. I also told him I have the utmost confidence in Hampton PD. And don't worry Chief, I wouldn't have said it if it wasn't true. Even though you haven't had a murder in over 10 years, it's basic investigative skills."

"Thanks Steve, that's much appreciated, we're getting good support from state," and Mark went on to update the Attorney General on the tip about the Mercury Marquis and what his detectives were doing.

"We're also having Mike Simmons snap pictures of everyone who's going into the wake and we've assigned a real spit and polish officer to direct traffic," Mark added.

"That sounds good Chief. Well, it looks like you have the bases covered and are making progress. If there's nothing else, we have to get back to the office."

"Thanks Steve and we'll keep you informed."

"I'll walk you out," Mark said.

As they were leaving, Keshen turned towards the Deputy Chief and said, "I'll be in touch."

Wrenn just smiled and thought of course you will.

****

The day for all concerned was inconsequential. None of the Cushing siblings were called because of the wake and funeral, Mike Simmons was able to take pictures of everyone going in or coming out, Shawn re-interviewed people at the schools where Robert Cushing taught and there was nothing new from Amesbury or Newburyport police departments. Maloney even called Mass State police and they had nothing on Cushing.

"We have nothing new," Wrenn said, "So let's get back to basics. What are the motives for Murder?"

"The four L's," Mike Simmons said.

"Loot, Lust, Love or Loathing."

"Exactly, so let's look at it. I think we can eliminate love. This wasn't a mercy killing," Lally said.

"My feelings too," Wrenn said. "So that leaves lust, loot or loathing."

"Lall, you keep working on the Marquis, I'll give the Cushing siblings a call and talk to them. I'll ask Renny to ask his mom too. He and one or two of the other kids are staying with her. Shawn, get a subpoena from court and get the Cushing's bank statements. Let's see what his finances look like."

"I can do that and I'll find out from the Amesbury school district if he had direct deposit and what bank. That should be able to tell us if he had any money or gambling issues."

"Good," Wrenn answered.

"And Mike, I'm going to ask Renny to come in and bring the guest list from the wake, and we'll see if anything jumps out at us. I'll also broach the subject of the possibility of his father having an affair and being part of a love triangle. Until I get that, work with Lall and see if we can get anywhere on the Marquis."

"Got it."

"We'll have a quick meeting tomorrow morning to see if anything new happened overnight and then get right to work."

The day wasn't inconsequential for Bob McLaughlin. The last thing he wanted to do was direct traffic at the Cushing wake. He went home, hit the bottle hard and called in sick the next day.

****

After fielding Barbara Keshen's morning call the next day, Bill Wrenn called the Cushing residence.

"Hi Renny, it's Bill Wrenn."

"Hello Deputy Chief. Do you have any suspects on my father's killer?"

"No we don't and that's why I'm calling you. I have some questions, would you rather do them over the phone or in person. If in person, I could come there in an unmarked cruise or you can come to the station, whatever you would like. Also, I'd like to take a look at the guest list for the wake and funeral."

"Why do you want that?"

"Like arsonists, murderers may want to view what they have done. I'm looking to see if any one name jumps out at you or me."

"I'll come to the station. My sister is here with my mom and you coming by would only disturb her. I'll be down in ten minutes."

"Thanks."

****

Renny was shown into Bill Wrenn's office and had a seat.

"Would you like a cup of coffee Renny?"

"No thanks we can get right to it. I brought the funeral guest list and I didn't see anyone who didn't like my father."

"Any names on the list you didn't recognize?"

"Yes there were."

"If you don't mind, I'd like to make a copy of the list and we'll do a record check on everyone to see if anything jumps out."

"I don't like that intrusion."

"Listen Renny, we're trying to solve your father's murder and we need to exhaust all avenues."

"What if I don't give to you?"

"I'll apply for a search warrant. I would like you to give it to me now and I'll have the chief's secretary copy it and give it back to you before you leave. I will also keep you appraised of anything we find or don't find."

Renny gave him the list.

"Excuse me one minute."

Wrenn took the list to the chief's secretary and asked her to make a copy of the list and then returned to his office and sat down.

"Renny I'm going to ask you some questions that you're not going to like. But if I don't explore these avenues I would be remiss."

"Go ahead."

"At our daily meeting, we went back to basics and looked at the various motives as to why people commit murders. I'm sorry to ask this question, but do you know if there was any chance that your father was having some sort of affair which would have led to some sort of love triangle."

Renny was obviously unhappy with the question.

"Deputy Chief Wrenn, there is absolutely no chance of that. My parents had an ideal marriage. They were the love of each other's life. I really resent that."

"I thought you would. My next questions will probably be as disturbing. But as I said, I'd be remiss if I didn't ask them."

"Did you know of any gambling or money problems your father may have had?"

"None whatsoever. My parents took vacations every year and paid for them in cash. They were planning a trip to Ireland in the fall and they had already saved the money for it. As for gambling, my dad wouldn't even buy a lottery ticket. He taught math and he knew the slim chances of winning."

Wrenn nodded his head.

"Last question. Did he ever receive any kind of threats, maybe from previous students he had or anyone else?"

Renny paused for a moment.

"My dad never received any kind of threats, but I have. Mainly because of some positions I've taken in the legislature and quite possibly because of my activities with the clamshell alliance and anti-nuclear and anti-war stance."

"How'd you get these threats?"

"Some came in the mail, and some phone calls. Actually my dad received a phone call with a threat about the Seabrook nuke, but it looks like it may have been directed at me. We're both in the phone book."

Bill Wrenn began to wonder if it could've been a case of mistaken identity, and Renny was the real target. It seemed there was no shortage of people who were upset at Renny and it was something that he would keep in the back of his mind. There was a knock on Wrenn's door.

"Come in."

It was the Chief's secretary with copies of the guest list. Bill gave the original to Renny and kept the copy.

"Well, that should about do it Renny, thank you for coming in. Unless you have any questions or anything else to offer, I'll walk you to the door."

"I can find my way out."

"I'm sure you can but the policy is no unattended guests in the station.

"Humph," was all Renny said in reply. He left the station without saying anything else.

****

After Renny left, Bill Wrenn called the Cushing siblings and asked if there was anyone upset with his father or people who disliked him or may have held a grudge. They all answered no.

****

That afternoon at the meeting, no one had anything significant to offer. Mike Simmons started.

"Chief, Lally and I got through most of the Marquis' that are registered in the surrounding counties. Pretty much all had alibis or just didn't fit the profile. We have several more to go, but nothing even close yet."

"Shawn you're next," Wrenn said.

"Cushing did his banking at the Hampton Co-op, right down the street from his house on Winnacunnet. I got the subpoenas and he had some intermittent large deposits since eighty-four. However, after checking with the realty company he worked for, they coincided with commissions from house sales he made. Outside of that, nothing unusual. I even checked to see if he had a safety deposit box, he doesn't."

"Any luck following up with Amesbury and Newburyport PD," Wrenn asked.

"No, I didn't have time. I'll get to it tomorrow."

"Okay, sounds good."

"That leaves me. I was able to get the guest list today from Renny, and I had one of the new specials running record checks. Nothing yet. However, Renny did bring up something interesting. He said that he's received a couple of death threats over the years from his activities in the clamshell alliance and his stances at the state house. At some point, we may have to look into if he was the intended target."

"Huh, that may be something," Lally said.

"All right, for tomorrow, Mike why don't you continue researching the owners of the Marquis' and Shawn hit Newburyport and Amesbury PD's. Lall, how are you doing on the Anderson case?"

Linda Anderson was a petite 5' 2" blonde who was a nurse. On the way to her car after work in mid-May, she was kidnapped and raped in Andover, Ma, by a man who she described as a tall, thin, black man. After multiple rapes and beatings, she was driven and left to die off of route 95 in Hampton by the toll booths. She was stabbed in the liver and her throat was cut. She would have died if it wasn't for a Good Samaritan who stopped, staunched the bleeding, and flagged down another car who stopped at the toll booths down the highway and called for an ambulance and state police.

"I haven't done anything on it since before the Cushing murder."

"Alright, spend some time on it today."

"Will do. I'll coordinate with Andover detectives and see if anything new popped up."

"Very good. See everyone tomorrow."

****

The next morning, Bill Wrenn brought Keshen up
to date on their lack of progress. He also told her that they
were looking into the possibility that Renny may have been
the target. Wrenn also told her that they had no definitive
suspects but were continuing their investigation.

That afternoon at the meeting, Wrenn and the
Hampton detectives had nothing more to offer.

"It looks like the Marquis is a dead end. We got
nothing today," Simmons said.

"Same thing at Newburyport and Amesbury PD's,
goose eggs," Maloney said.

"And I got nothing from Renny on who might want
to kill him except for every employee at the Seabrook
nuclear power plant. That would be somewhere around
seven hundred," Wrenn said.

"Lall, any luck on the Anderson case."

"Not a thing, outside of the fact that she described
the rapist as a tall thin black man, they don't have any
suspects. They have some transfer evidence from her
clothes, but no fingerprints. They also have evidence from
the rape kit if we can find a suspect but right now, Andover
has no suspects."

"Alright, let's meet tomorrow and plan on which
way to go."

****

Next day's meeting was morose. No one had anything to offer or which direction to go.

"I thought we'd have this solved by now," Wrenn said.

"Join the club," Simmons said.

"Any suggestions?"

The detectives looked at each other.

"So it's back to where we started," Wrenn said.

"Lall, split your day between the two cases and let's re-interview everyone we've already talked to. Mike, try to get faces paired with names from the guest list and I'll call the siblings again."

As Wrenn entered his office, his phone began to ring. He checked the caller ID before picking up the receiver.

"Hello Barbara."

"Good morning Deputy Chief.

Wrenn then brought the assistant AG up to speed on this morning's meeting.

"You mean to tell me that you don't have one suspect and you're no closer to solving the murder than the night of the murder."

"I mean to tell you that we've eliminated a number of individuals as suspects and we're continuing our investigation."

"Deputy Chief Wrenn, you're just not doing enough."

"We've conducted investigations before Barbara and we're doing everything that there is to do. You cannot get blood from a stone, but Barbara please," Wrenn said getting exasperated, "If you have anything to offer on what to do, please, please let me know, I'll be more than happy to investigate that particular avenue."

There was silence from the other end of the phone.

"Please keep me appraised of what's going on. Goodbye Deputy Chief."

"Goodbye Barbara."

To say that the conversation was somewhat contentious would have been an understatement.

****

The next two weeks dragged for the investigators at Hampton. They continued their investigation and were getting nowhere. Bill Lally and the Andover detectives also had no suspects on the kidnap and rape of Linda Anderson

When Bill Lally came into his office on Monday, June 20, he had a note to call one of the caretakers at the Town cemetery, Stacy Weeks. Stacy was well liked, a good worker and always had a smile on his face.

"Hi Stacy, this is Bill Lally at the PD. What's up?"

"Hi Bill. I not sure if this means anything, but when I was doing my rounds at the cemetery, I noticed that there was a broken beer bottle on Robert Cushing's grave."

"Really. Stacy, after you hang up, can you get someone to stand by the grave and not touch anything, and make sure no one else touches anything? I'll be right there."

"You bet Bill."

Bill told Mike Simmons and grabbed his fingerprint kit and camera. Before they left, they stopped at Bill Wrenn's office and told him about Stacy's call.

"It would be great if we got some prints from the broken bottle fragments. If I remember correctly, the headstone is just porous stone without a polished surface," Wrenn said.

"That's right chief, nothing on the headstone is polished and it just has the last name. If I'm not mistaken, it's a family plot and can hold up to four bodies," Lally answered.

"Let me know how you make out."

****

The daily phone calls from Barbara Keshen had tapered off and her calls were every two or three days. Wrenn decided to call her.

"Hello Barbara, this is Bill."

"Hello Chief, since you're calling me I suspect you have something."

"Yes, we received a report from one of the cemetery staff that someone broke a beer bottle over Cushing's headstone."

"Well, send someone to try and dust for prints."

"Thank you Barbara, but that's already been done. We know what to do and what not to do," Wrenn said while shaking his head.

Keshen seemed not to notice Wrenn's response.

"Make sure you dust the gravestone for prints too."

Wrenn gripped the phone a little tighter.

"Barbara, the stone has no polished surfaces. It's one-hundred percent porous. You can't lift fingerprints from a porous surface."

"Chief please, just try."

"Barbara, like blood, you can't get prints from a stone. But if it makes you happy. Goodbye Barbara. If we get anything from the bottles I'll let you know the results."

"Goodbye Chief."

Wrenn complimented himself on not saying what he was thinking.

To be on the safe side, Wrenn called the state lab and spoke to one of the fingerprint experts to see if there was a new technology that he was unaware of that would in fact, lift prints from a porous surface. The state's lead crime scene investigator confirmed what Wrenn already knew, you can't get fingerprints from a porous stone surface.

Authors note: In the 1980's, the technology didn't exist to lift fingerprints from unpolished stone. By the mid 1990's, studies have shown that the use of black magnetic powder for nonporous stones and the use of ninhydrin for porous stones yielded fingerprints of good evidentiary value. The FBI also developed a laser procedure in the 1990's to lift latent fingerprints from all porous surfaces.

****

"Headquarters to 37, Sergeant Simmons. Can you please call in for Chief Wrenn when you get to the cemetery?"

"Ten-five," Simmons answered as Bill Lally was driving.

"What's that about?"

"Not sure but I'll call when we get to the cemetery.

Lally pulled into the cemetery and into a parking space by the office and main building.

"Hi Stacy, how's it going? Okay if I use the phone? I have to call the station."

"No problem Bill. When are you guys going to get one of those portable bag phones?"

"Not for a while, they're over one-thousand dollars."

"Wow."

Bill called Wrenn's number directly.

"Hi Chief, it's Lall."

"You're not going to believe this."

"What?"

"Keshen wants us to try and take prints from the headstone."

"You're kidding right? You did tell her it's porous?"

"Oh yea, you try talking to her."

Bill started laughing.

"No problem Chief and we'll even take pictures of the headstone with powder on it."

"Thanks Bill, let me know how you make out."

Lally then told Simmons the gist of the call.

"She's a pip isn't she?"

"She certainly is. So Stacy, what do you have."

"I figured I'd call you guys. Someone broke a beer bottle on Cushing's grave and there's a wet spot on it."

"Huh. Did someone piss on his grave or was it just let over beer from the bottle?" Lally asked.

"Don't know Bill, maybe either."

All three got into the detectives car and drove to the Cushing grave.

When they arrived at the grave, Bill put gloves on, collected the broken shards of the bottle and put them in a paper evidence bag. Paper was used instead of plastic so they wouldn't be a buildup of condensation on the glass inside a plastic bag.

"Where's the wet spot Stacy," Maloney asked.

"It's gone. It must have evaporated. It was somewhere on the top of the grave to the middle."

"Well it's not there now. Too bad. If it was urine we could have gotten some evidence from it, like what blood type."

"Too bad it wasn't on the ground. We could've taken some of the dirt and analyzed that," Lally said.

"Let's waste our time now and dust the rock."

"Will you guys need me anymore?" Stacy asked.

"No we'll be all set. Thanks much Stacy and if you should see anything unusual, don't be bashful and call."

"Will do guys."

Lally then dusted the gravestone while Simmons took pictures.

As expected, no prints were lifted from the headstone.

Back at the station, Lally dusted the beer bottle shards and was unable to lift any prints. He went to Wrenn's office to break the news.

"No luck Chief. We got some smudges and blurs, but nothing we can use."

"I'm just thinking Lall, let's assume for a second that the wet spot Stacy saw on the grave was urine and the guy wore gloves. He was dancing and pissing on

Cushing's grave, and if that's the case, then loathing was
definitely the motive. How 'bout the type of beer."

"Unknown Chief, the labels were peeled off."

After a moment's thought, Wrenn said, "Well it
could've been kids and the busted beer bottle was random,
or it could've been the killer. Before the day's over, you
and Shawn rattle some doors on Emery Lane and George
road and see if anyone heard or saw anything." Both roads
abutted the cemetery.

"No problem. I already checked the log for last
night and we had no noise complaints or anything else in
the area."

"Thanks."

****

By the end of the day, after canvassing the
neighborhood by the cemetery, the detectives came up with
goose eggs again, and that continued throughout the rest of
the month.

****

*Authors note: When the Chief and detectives were
interviewed, none remembered the color of the broken beer
bottle. If the shards were green, it's possible that the bottle
could've been Lowenbrau, and the person could've been
McLaughlin. It remains one of the unanswered questions
of the case.*

Chapter 6
The Investigation, July

It was July 2 and the "murderer's circle" of hazing was in full gear in the locker room at Hampton PD. There was also talk of the Cushing murder.

Out of the blue, Lee Griffen turned towards McLaughlin and said, "You did it, didn't you Bob. I heard the other day you arrested Cushing in the seventies and he came after you and tried to get you fired. This is payback isn't it? Come on, confess Bob, it's good for the soul."

"Everyone's a comedian," McLaughlin answered.

"And Lee, I hear you're a virgin too. I got someone who will make a man out of you," McLaughlin countered.

"Don't screw with the Mongoose," another cop said to Griffen, "He'll seal you faith."

The banter continued.

Detective Phil Russell was in the locker room too and as he was leaving, he noticed that McLaughlin left his locker open. As he went to close it, he noticed that a sawed off shotgun that McLaughlin kept in his locker wasn't there. No big deal he thought, he probably put it in the department's evidence locker. Phil seemed to remember that he had seized it on a previous case and it should be in evidence anyway.

After the shift ended that night, McLaughlin hit the bottle.

****

The 4th of July is the busiest time of year for the Hampton Police Department as people flock to the beach for their summer vacation. The population swells to well over one-hundred thousand. That year was particularly busy since the 4th fell on a Monday, so in addition to families taking a week-long vacation, there were many who took long weekends. All the hotel rooms were booked and the Hampton Police made over three-hundred arrests. Most of the arrests were alcohol related, however there were a number of felonies that detectives needed to follow-up and investigate. Fortunately there were two other detectives in the division that summer who could handle the bulk of those cases while Lally, Maloney and Simmons spent time on the McLaughlin murder and the Anderson kidnapping and rape.

Shortly after the 4th, Bill Wrenn had a meeting with his detectives.

"So where are we?" Wrenn asked.

"Chief, we're absolutely nowhere. We have nothing," Simmons answered.

"Lall, are you anywhere on the Anderson case?"

"Nowhere, Andover PD even got the Eagle Tribune to write an article on the case and ask for help if anyone saw or heard anything."

"They get anything?" Wrenn asked.

"They got a few calls, but nothing panned out."

"Hmmm, let's do it," Wrenn said.

"Do what?"

"I'll run it by Chief Mark first, but let's contact the local papers, The Hampton Union, the Union Leader, etc., and do the same thing. We'll ask the public for help on both the Anderson and Cushing case. Did anyone see anything or did anyone hear anyone talking about it?"

"It's a long shot, but yea, we don't have much else," Simmons said. Both Lally and Mahoney nodded agreement.

"If Mark okay's it Chief, why don't you call them. A deputy Chief will have more influence as opposed to a detective Sergeant calling."

"Alright, I'll go talk to Bob Mark now."

Chief Mark gave his approval and the article ran the next day in the local papers.

****

During the second week of July, they caught a break on the McLaughlin case thanks to the newspaper article.

"Hampton Police, may I help you?"

"Yes please. I may have some information on the Cushing murder. Can I speak to someone in detectives?"

"Right away sir. May I have your name and number in case we get disconnected?"

"Sure, my name is Mike Gallo, and my number is 603-555-1212."

"Thank you Mister Gallo. I'll put you right through."

"Detectives, Detective Lally."

"Hello Detective, my name is Mike Gallo and I may have some information for you concerning the Cushman murder."

"Thank you, what do you have?" Bill asked.

"Well, I work at the Seabrook nuke and sometime in May, before Robert Cushing was killed, a co-worker of mine, who's kind of a jerk, said that he wanted to kill Renny Cushing because he's been trying to shut us down with the Clamshell Alliance and some laws he's been trying to pass in the state House, and you know, that's a living for us workers. As you can probably guess, there aren't too many people here at the nuke who like Cushing."

"What's this co-worker's name?"

"His name is James Adams and he works the second shift."

"What time is that shift?"

"He works four to midnight plus some overtime."

"Do you have his phone number or know where he lives."

"I don't know his number, but I'm pretty sure he lives in Somersworth."

"Thanks Mike. Would you mind coming in and giving us a voluntary statement?"

"I really don't want to get that involved. If he finds out it's me he may want to get back at me."

"I understand. How about if you give me some information where I can contact you in the future."

After Gallo gave Lally his information, Bill thanked him and assured Gallo that unless it was an emergency, he wouldn't contact him at work so he wouldn't be compromised.

"What was that?" Simmons asked after Lally hung up.

"Just got a call from a Mike Gallo. He works at the nuke. He said that one of his co-workers, a James Adams, threatened to kill Renny Cushing in early May before Robert Cushing was murdered."

"Really, who is this guy?" Simmons asked.

"Gallo thinks he lives in Somersworth and he works the second shift. Maybe we can catch him at home today."

"Sounds good Lall. You and Mahoney do a background on this guy, contact Somersworth PD, see what they got, and I'll let Wrenn know."

****

Later that morning at 10 AM, there was a meeting in Chief Wrenn's office which was also attended by Phil Russell. Phil was a seasoned and competent detective who helped with the Cushing case on and off in the past month in addition to working other cases.

"What do you have Lall?" Wrenn asked.

"Adams does in fact live in Somersworth and we have an address. Mahoney checked with Somersworth PD and outside of motor vehicle offenses, the most serious being a DWI, that's it for a record. He's also on record as being a gun owner. I checked with Fish and Game and he has a hunting license. He's thirty years old."

"So there is a possibility that Renny was the target and this was either mistaken identity or the elder Cushing was shot as punishment. Let's do this," Wrenn said.

"Phil, you and Shawn go interview Adams after checking in with Somersworth PD. Mike you head over to the nuke and check with the HR department. See what they have on him. Lall, don't you have a meeting today with Andover detectives on the Anderson case."

"Yea I do."

"Okay do that and I'll bring Bob Mark up to date and then I'll call Renny to see if he knows this guy."

****

"Hi Renny, it's Bill Wrenn."

"Hello Deputy Chief, what can I do for you?"

"We received some intelligence that someone by the name of James Adams made a death threat against you in early May. Do you know of anyone by that name?"

After a moment's hesitation, Renny said, "No I don't. You don't think he was serious, do you?"

"I'm not sure. But it's something we need to check out. Now if I'm not mistaken, you're still working with the Clamshell Alliance."

"That's correct. Can you check with some of the others running the organization and see if they recognize the name?"

"I can do that."

Renny called Chief Wrenn the next day and advised him that no one was familiar with that name.

****

After Mike Simmons came back from the Human Resource department at the Seabrook Nuclear plant, he walked into Bill Wrenn's office.

"Anything from HR?"

"Not a thing. He's off the radar. No discipline and average amount of sick days. The only blip was he was on a scheduled day off the night of the murder."

"Okay, we'll see what Phil digs up."

****

It was 11:30 AM when Russell knocked on the door of James Adam's apartment. He was with Shawn Mahoney and Somersworth detective, Mark Prescott.

Adams opened the door wearing a stained white t-shirt and baggy cargo shots. He had hair down to his shoulders and was smoking a cigarette.

"Hello James Adams."

"Yea, who are you?"

"I'm detective Russell from Hampton PD, this is Shawn Mahoney also from Hampton and detective Mark Prescott from Somersworth. Can we come in and ask you a few questions?"

Adams just turned and walked to his kitchen table and sat down.

"Yea, c'mon in. What's this all about?"

"We're investigating the murder of Robert Cushing in Hampton. Can you tell us where you were the night of June 1st this year?"

"No I can't."

"Do you not know?"

"I know where I was. It's none of your business."

Russell wasn't surprised at the answer. He had gotten that before from suspects in other cases, though it was the first time in this case. So he tried another tack.

"Do you know Renny Cushing?"

"I know of him. I don't know him personally."

"We have information that in early May, you made threats that you were going to kill him."

"Who told you that?"

"We don't reveal sources," Russell said and then added to throw Adams off, "But it was more than one. Seeing that Cushing's father was killed shortly thereafter, that's why we're here."

"I don't know Renny Cushing or his father and no one at the nuke likes him or his organization, the Clamshell Alliance. He's trying to take away our livelihood. At one time or the other, everyone at the nuke has said they want to kill him. It's just talk, nothing more."

"When we did a background check on you, we noticed you have a hunting license. Do you own a shotgun?" Russell asked.

"Yea, I do. I also have a long gun. A Remington .308 bolt action."

"Can we take the shotgun with us so we can do a ballistics test on it?"

"No you can't."

"Listen James, you're a prime suspect at the moment. What we call a person of interest, and I suspect you don't like cops. If you didn't do the murder, the quickest way to get rid of us is to cooperate. You don't want to give us your shotgun, that's fine. But then we'll go and get a search warrant for it, and while we're doing this, we'll station two uniformed officers here to make sure you don't do anything to hide evidence. You want to call a lawyer, that's fine too."

After a moment's thought Adams said, "Alright, I'll get the shotgun."

As he went into his bedroom, he was followed by detective Prescott. Adams looked at him, but surprisingly did or said nothing.

As Adams handed Prescott the gun, Prescott checked to see if the safety was on, which it was and then checked to see if it was unloaded, which it was.

"How long will you have it?" Adams asked.

"It should be about a week. We'll drive it up to the state police lab and then do a ballistics test, and then drive back here and give it to you," Russell answered. He didn't add what he was thinking that if the test showed a match, he'd be back, but with an arrest warrant.

"Thank you James," Russell said.

As he was walking out, Russell turned to Adams and said as an afterthought, "If you really want to get rid of us James, you can take a polygraph."

"And it can be at the Somersworth PD so you don't have to travel to Hampton," Prescott said.

"I didn't do it but I don't trust lie detectors," Adams answered.

"Listen, unless you agree to it, it can't be used against you. Call your lawyer. But if you didn't do it and passed, we'd be out of your hair."

"I'll think about it."

"Here's my card, if you decide to do it call me and we'll get it set up at your convenience," Prescott said.

The following day after talking to his lawyer, Adams agreed to the polygraph.

****

Authors note: A polygraph has four sensors. It monitors the persons breathing, pulse, blood pressure and perspiration (galvanic skin response). Generally, when a person is lying, all increase relative to a resting state. When the polygraph test starts, the questioner asks three or four simple questions to establish the norms for the person's signals. Then the real questions being tested by the polygraph are asked. Throughout questioning, all of the person's signals are recorded on the moving paper.

When a well-trained examiner uses a polygraph, he or she can detect lying with high accuracy. However, because the examiner's interpretation is subjective and because different people react differently to lying, a polygraph test is not perfect and can be fooled. One of the key reasons a polygraph is not called a lie detector test is because the results aren't as simple as pass or fail. Some subjects taking a polygraph find themselves with inconclusive test results. An inconclusive test can be a result of a number of factors such as: the improper formulation of questions by the examiner, the lack of fear by the examinee, the issue is of little or no consequence, or, if they are not in a controlled environment where outside noise and distractions are minimized.

An example of an improper question would be the following: when a professional examiner asks, "Did you cause your girlfriend to go missing?" The reason for this is because if you sent your girlfriend to the shop and she didn't return, you might believe it was your fault for sending her. The question should be "Do you know where you girlfriend is now?"

****

Dave Ford was the NH State Trooper who gave James Adams the polygraph test at Somersworth PD. He had recently graduated from the Royal Canadian Mounted Police Federal Polygraph School. He was also a graduate of St. Anslem's college with a BA in Criminal Justice.

It was Thursday July 21st and he was at the Hampton police station meeting with Chief Wrenn, Phil Russell and Sergeant Simmons.

"No doubt about it. Adams passed the polygraph."

It was not the answer Wrenn was hoping to get.

"Any areas where it could be inconclusive?" Russell asked.

"Not at all. He was straight forward and wasn't worried. Take a look at this," Ford said while pointing to the polygraph readout.

"When I asked him if he had anything to do with the murder of Robert Cushing, it was a classic non-deceptive response. He has this one big breath and his breathing slows, no GSR response and his blood pressure actually goes down. It's a text book truthful response."

Wrenn just shook his head.

"Aren't there some people who can beat the polygraph?" Wrenn asked.

"There are, but the results usually come back as inconclusive, and when we asked them to take a second test, they generally refuse, not so with Adams."

"Thanks Dave it's really appreciated."

"No problem Chief, if you need anything else, just contact us. We know how important this case is. Do you have any other suspects?"

"At this point no."

"Good luck then."

"Well, we're still waiting on the ballistics results on the shotgun. "If that comes back as a hit, it could get interesting," Simmons said.

"Yea, I called the lab today and they said they should have the results tomorrow," Wrenn answered.

The lab result came back the following day which was a Friday, and it was negative. In other words, the ballistics didn't match up to the slugs that killed Robert Cushing. Whereas Adams could've been lying and beat the polygraph, ballistics don't lie. Adams didn't kill Cushing.

Wrenn got on the phone to Barbara Keshen and told her the recent case developments.

****

The following Monday, Tim Collins was in detectives talking to Bill Lally when they were joined by Bob McLaughlin.

"So Bill what do you have on the Cushing murder and how you guys doing?" McLaughlin asked.

Lally shook his head. "Bob, we don't have a fucking thing. We're no closer to solving this case then we were on the night Cushing was murdered. Literally, the only physical evidence we have is the two bullet holes in the screen door, and the only other thing we have is some nebulous description that the possible shooter was a young man with dirty blonde hair wearing purple shorts. That's it."

"Keep plugging Lall, we got faith in you," McLaughlin said.

McLaughlin turned and left Lally's office. Halfway down the hall, Tim Collins heard and eerie laugh from McLaughlin. It reminded him of the Vincent Price laugh from the Michael Jackson music video, Thriller.

That night, McLaughlin told his wife about the conversation with Lally.

****

Handy Dan's was located at 650 Lafayette road in Hampton and it was a popular combination deli and coffee shop. Their coffee came in several flavors from the Piscataqua Coffee Roasting Company. They were also the only store in town that carried Boers Head meats.

Bob McLaughlin usually came in on Saturdays when it wasn't as busy as during the week. He came right after roll call where it was announced that James Adams passed the polygraph test and that there were no viable suspects.

Colon Forbes, who lived in Hampton, had been a New Hampshire State Trooper for a little over ten years and was assigned to the major crimes unit of state police. Essentially, he was an upper grade detective that investigated murders and all other serious crimes in the state. He was well respected by his peers and other police agencies in the state, and also by Bob McLaughlin.

"Colon, how you doing," Bob said.

"Good Bob, let me grab a coffee and bagel and I'll join you."

After getting his order, Colon sat at the table with McLaughlin.

"How's everything going Bob?"

"Not bad, but the stress of the job gets to you. I'm looking forward to retirement. I was doing karate for a while and that helped, but I stopped"

"How many years do you have in?" Forbes asked.

"Eighteen and a half, and I'll be retiring as soon as I hit twenty."

"Hey listen Bob, I fish a lot and that really relaxes me. Why don't you try it sometime? I've got some extra rods and we can go together."

"Thanks Colon. I think I'll take you up on that."

Just then McLaughlin's portable radio squawked.

"Headquarters to 306, respond to the intersection of High street and Lafayette road, there's a ten twenty five, three cars, with PI. Fire ambulance is responding."

Dispatch just assigned McLaughlin a motor vehicle accident with personal injury.

"Oh well Colon, duty calls."

"See you later Mongoose."

McLaughlin smiled as he went out the door. He liked that nickname.

****

Robert McLaughlin junior was living with his mom Beverly, the senior McLaughlin's divorced wife, in Seabrook. NH. It was the last week of July when he got a call from his father. They hadn't seen each other for some time and it seemed like his Dad was trying to make amends. He liked that. They had never been very close and junior liked the fact that his dad was reaching out to him.

When junior arrived, both he and senior embraced. Sammi had gone out on an errand. Junior noticed that his Dad was drinking, but wasn't drunk. Senior was touched that his son came over after not seeing him for nearly a year.

Senior then said to his son, "I trust you and I appreciate you wanting to re-establish a relationship with me. I'm going to show you how much I trust you by telling you something that can get me in a lot of trouble. I will essentially, put my life in your hands."

Senior then told his son, the events of June first and how he killed Robert Cushing. He also told him of the thirteen year grudge he held against Cushing. He told junior how Sammi had intervened and planned the murder and the disguises so he wouldn't get caught. Junior told his father that he could be trusted and wouldn't tell a soul.

****

About ten minutes after McLaughlin confessed to his son, Sammi came in.

"Hi Bobby, what a pleasant surprise. It's good to see you," she said.

"You too Sammi, it's been a while."

"Hey Sammi, I want you to know I told Bobby everything about murdering Cushing," senior said.

Sammi was temporarily stunned. "Why did you do that?"

Senior then said, "We know that we can trust him. I know that I can trust him. He's my son and I know he wouldn't do anything to hurt us."

Sammi became very pensive and after a minute's thought she said, "You're right. If you can't trust family, who can you trust?"

Sammi went on to tell junior that what his dad told him was true. She then went on to describe the roll that she played in the murder, by coming up with the plan, disguising themselves and how she purposely walked in front of a car so she could be seen. She then said to junior, "I'm not worried about being caught Bobby because it has been nearly two months since the murder, and the only clue the police have is a description of a young man wearing purple shorts carrying a stick. The gun is long gone and they'll never find it."

After a short while, junior left the apartment but came back that night. It was agreed that he would live with them for a period of time. Junior lived with his dad and Sammi for the next three weeks. He left only after his father's drinking became too much to take.

Chapter 7
The Investigation, August

July merged into August and the Hampton Police had no viable suspects. A number of other persons were investigated who didn't like Renny Cushing, but as Adams had said, it was just talk.

Bob McLaughlin was in the supervisor's office at the station talking to John Campbell.

"So what do you think Sarge, are we going to get this guy who killed Cushing?"

After a moment's thought, Campbell replied.

"Bob, the only way we're going to get this guy is if he gets drunk one night, feels guilty, and then confesses; because, right now, we got nothing."

****

During the second week of August, Barbara Keshen called Bill Wrenn.

"Hello Deputy Chief, It's Barbara."

"Hello Barbara, what can I do for you?"

"About a month ago when the investigation was stalling, we had one of our investigators contact the FBI and ask them to do a profile on Robert Cushing's killer, and we just got the results back."

"What do we have?" Wrenn said.

"Nothing too surprising. Given the description of the young man with slicked back hair we have from witnesses, they said we should be looking at one of his past students."

"Your right, that's not too surprising."

"Do you think you can have your detectives go back to where he taught school and look at past students who would now be in their late teens to early twenties."

"That's viable. I'll assign Maloney and Simmons, and we'll do record checks to see if anyone stands out."

"Thanks Deputy Chief."

****

For the next three days, Simmons and Maloney ran background checks on all Cushing's male students who would now be eighteen to twenty-five. They found nothing of significance.

Authors note: The FBI's Behavior Analysis Unit was created in the mid 1980's. It was then known as the National Center for the Analysis of Violent Crime (NCAVC). They receive requests for services from federal, state, local, and international law enforcement agencies for assistance in giving a possible psychological and sometimes physical profile of a killer, particularly serial killers. They are generally very accurate on their assessments. One of its original investigators, John Douglas, wrote a book titled Mind Hunters.

****

It was midafternoon when McLaughlin had his first Lowenbrau. He looked out his back window and saw Marie Cushing walking through her backyard when she sat down on a two person swing that she and her husband use to sit on together. She started to cry.

McLaughlin knew he was responsible for her grief. He began to tear up when he decided to have his first shot of vodka and for the first time, he began regretting his actions of June 1.

****

It was 7:15 AM and John Campbell had just finished morning roll call on Tuesday, August 23rd when Chief Mark entered the room. Sergeant Rick Mathews was also on duty.

"John, it's Chief Oliverira's funeral in Salisbury today. We have four motorcycles from our honor guard going. Can you send someone with a cruiser too?" Mark said. Chief Oliveira was a retired Police Chief from Salisbury, Ma.

"No problem Chief. If I'm not mistaken, the funeral starts at ten AM and it's just a quick service. I'll send someone with the supervisor's car and make sure they will be there by nine thirty. It was just washed and vacuumed before the shift."

"Thanks, let me know if there are any problems."

Campbell turned towards McLaughlin.

"Bob, you're looking good as usual. If you have nothing going, why don't you take the detail?

"I can do that. All my reports are up to date and I'm caught up on everything else. I'll coordinate with the four motor guys"

"Good," Campbell answered.

To be given the supervisors car was a privilege that most patrolman envied. Whenever a patrolman acted as a supervisor, they were given starting Sergeants pay. It was referred to as Temporary Service out of Rank.

When McLaughlin arrived at the funeral home, he was met by an acquaintance, Captain Roger Goudreau of Salisbury PD.

"Hi Bob, how's it going?"

"Good cap, you."

"Not bad. I really hate these things."

"The family is having a short ceremony at the funeral home and then we'll have a procession to the Longhill Cemetery. We're going to have a Salisbury cruiser lead the procession followed by the hearse and the family car. Why don't you and the motors fall in behind the family car. You guys are looking good."

"We can do that."

"Listen, after the cemetery, we're having a get together for the officers attending that is separate from the family mercy meal."

"Thanks, I'll let the others know, but I have to head back to the station, I'm working a day shift."

"Okay, I've already thanked him, but thank Chief Mark again for me."

"Absolutely."

Thirty minutes later, McLaughlin saw Chief Oliveira's widow being helped to the family car because of her grief. The ride to the Longhill Cemetery took about fifteen minutes plus another twenty to form around the grave. After the eulogy was said at the grave, taps were played and there was a flyover by the Mass State Police Helicopter. McLaughlin and the four motorcycle cops stood at attention and saluted. The widow continued to wail and McLaughlin realized the grief he was putting Marie Cushing through. It gnawed at his gut and he had extreme feelings of guilt. These guilt feelings started earlier in the month and wouldn't go away. He was regretting what he had done.

****

After the funeral, McLaughlin headed back to the station where he saw Rick Mathews. Rick noticed that his friend looked preoccupied.

"What's the matter Bobby?"

"Ahh, you know Rick, these cop funerals really suck."

"Yea, I know exactly what you mean. You can't help but picture yourself in that casket and the grief that it would cause your family. I go to them, but it doesn't get any easier. Don't worry, it will pass."

"Thanks Rick. If it's okay, I'm going to go on my lunch break before I resume patrol.

"No problem, and can you do me a favor and grab me a coffee?"

"No problem Rick."

After his lunch break, McLaughlin got his Sergeant and best friend a coffee, and then resumed patrol.

****

"Hey Sarge, you may want to take this call," the on
duty dispatcher yelled to Mathews.

"What is it?"

"Some guy travelling south on route 95, north of the
tolls, just had a shotgun pointed at him by a guy in another
car. I already sent McLaughlin out to look for him."

Mathews wondered if this could have any relation
to the Cushing case. This may be the break everyone was
waiting for.

"Good. Send Joe Galvin out there too," Mathews
thought to himself that these are two of his best officers.

"Okay sarge."

When McLaughlin got the call, he was on Exeter
road, not far from route 95. He couldn't get the grief of
Oliveira's widow and Marie Cushing out of his mind. The
last thing he wanted to do was go to a gun call. He thought
he needed a drink or two or ten. He saw a payphone,
pulled over and called the direct line into the supervisor's
office.

"Sergeant Mathews speaking."

"Hey Rick, it's Bobby. I feel terrible. My stomach
is killing me. Is it okay if I go home?

Mathews thought that McLaughlin must really be
sick to not go on a call.

"Sure Bobby no problem. We'll send someone
else."

Before Mathews could send someone else, John Campbell, the street supervisor, called in that he was also responding to route 95.

Neither Galvin nor Campbell were able to locate the car and there were no further reports of a shotgun wielding driver.

McLaughlin went to the station, went right to his car, went home and started drinking.

He woke up the next day and called in sick and started drinking. He did the same thing on Thursday and Friday.

It was two PM on Friday when Sammi became very worried that her husband might commit suicide. She called the station and asked for Rick Mathews. After finding out he was on a day off, he called him at home.

****

"Hi Rick, it's Sammi."

"Sammi, what's wrong? Why are you crying?"

"Rick, you need to come down here, Bobby's in bad shape."

"I'll be there in ten minutes."

Rick then called out to his wife to tell her why he's going out, got into his car, and drove to McLaughlin's apartment on Elsie Street.

****

When Mathews got to the apartment building, he saw Sammi on the outside steps smoking a cigarette.

"Sammi what's going on?"

"It's Bobby, he hasn't stopped drinking since he left work sick the other day."

"Why's he on such a bender?"

Sammi knew that it was guilt over the Cushing murder but told Rick, "I don't know, he was shook up over that funeral."

"Alright let's go in and I'll talk to him."

When they got in, McLaughlin was at the table drinking vodka straight. There was an empty beer bottle on the table in addition to some prescription drug vials that were open. Mathews could see that his friend was very intoxicated. Sammi sat down on the couch.

Mathews sat down at the table and said, "What's wrong Bobby?"

McLaughlin put the vodka bottle in front of Mathews and asked, "Do you want a drink Rick."

"No, I'm all set Bobby and you should probably take it easy."

"Why don't you go home Rick?"

"I'm not going anywhere Bobby until you tell me what's eating you."

"Do you love me Rick?"

"Of course, I love you like a brother Bobby. We've been through thick and thin together for seventeen years, ever since I got on the PD."

McLaughlin just looked at Mathews. He then extended his right arm with his index finger pointed at the Cushing house. Mathews was puzzled. McLaughlin did it a second time and this time hit his right arm with his left hand as he extended his finger.

Mathews looked at where McLaughlin was pointing which was out the window.

Mathews got up and walked to the window and looked outside.

"Bobby, is that the Cushing house you're pointing to?"

McLaughlin didn't say anything. Mathews then remembered the arrest of Cushing and how Cushing tried to have him and McLaughlin fired after they arrested Gladys Ring.

"No Bobby. You didn't kill Cushing, did you?"

"Do you love me now Rick?"

"I'll always love you Bobby."

McLaughlin just looked at Mathews and said nothing. He said to Sammi, "Go ahead babe, tell him, tell Rick."

"I thought we weren't going to tell anybody Bobby."

"Tell him babe."

"I tried to stop him Rick. I tried really hard with my karate stick that night, but I couldn't."

"That's right Rick, I offed him."

"Alright Bobby, stop drinking right know we're going to go see Dr Seemans. We need to get you some help." Dr Seemans was the acting department psychiatrist. He was currently at Pease Air Force Base hospital in Portsmouth NH.

After calling Doctor Seemans who was at the hospital and telling him he had an emergency with McLaughlin, Seemans agreed to see them.

****

On the way to the hospital, McLaughlin confessed to Mathews again.

"He's the reason I never went anywhere in the department. That's why I whacked him."

Mathews thought of something and said, "Bobby, we got a description of a young man in purple shots. Who was that?"

McLaughlin hesitated. "That was probably Sammi Rick. She tried to stop me."

Rick just nodded his head. He was still shocked.

****

When they got to the hospital, they went to Doctor Seeman's office and McLaughlin was admitted right away.

After McLaughlin went into the Doctor's office, Mathews call Skip Bateman.

"Hi Rick, what's the matter," Bateman could tell from Mathews's voice that something was wrong.

"It's Bobby, he's in a bad way and I'm at the Pease Hospital. He's in with Dr Seemans now. Can you come up here?"

"No problem, I'll be there in about twenty minutes."

"See you then."

"Okay, I'll be waiting."

When Bateman got there, he met Mathews in Dr. Seemans waiting room.

"What's up Rick?"

"Bobby's in bad shape. He's pretty drunk and has been taking pills. He just admitted to me that he's the one who killed Cushing."

Bateman was stunned. He almost asked if he was serious, but he knew Rick was.

"Do you think he really did it?"

"I don't know Skip. That's one of the reasons I brought him here. If he didn't, he's protecting someone who did."

"You don't think it was Sammi, do you?" Bateman answered,

"I just don't know. This is the worst thing that has happened to me in my police career."

****

"Have a seat Bob," Doctor Seemans said, and then continued, "Rick brought you in and said you needed to talk."

"I'm not going there, I've said enough Doc."

"I understand how you feel Bob, but you've opened up to me before and taken me into your deepest confidence. Something big is bothering you. You need to open up."

McLaughlin hesitated, and then told Doctor Seemans everything. Seemans was surprised to hear about the arrest of Cushing in 1975 and how McLaughlin held a thirteen year grudge against him. He thought it particularly troubling and macabre that he moved in next to Cushing.

When the Doctor came out of the room, Mathews knew that McLaughlin had confessed to him. The Doctor nodded his head.

"Rick, I believe he's telling you the truth."

Mathews looked down.

"Hey Rick," McLaughlin said, "You need to take me in."

"I'm going to have to call Bill Wrenn Bobby."

"I know."

"Rick, go to the car with Bobby, I'll call Wrenn," Bateman said.

As Rick walked McLaughlin out the door, Bateman called Chief Wrenn.

Wrenn had just walked through his door when he heard the phone ring.

"Hey Bill, its Skip."

"Hi Skip, what's wrong."

"I'm not sure how to say this, but Bob McLaughlin killed Cushing. He confessed to Rick earlier today and then Doctor Seemans. We're at Pease hospital now and we're on our way back to the station."

"Alright, I'll see you there. I gotta call Bob Mark, State Police and the AG's office.

"I'll see you there Chief."

"Listen Skip, when you get to the station, put Bob in the interview room and make sure that someone's with him always."

"Will do."

After Wrenn called Chief Mark, he called Barbara Keshen who was in the office.

"Yes Deputy Chief."

"It looks like we're making an arrest on the Cushing case. We got a confession earlier today. Details are sketchy right now, but after I call State Police, I'm on my way into the station."

"Why are you calling State Police? Do you have some evidence that needs to be processed?"

"No Barbara. I'm calling State Police because they need to take over the investigation from here. The person who confessed to the murder is Hampton Police Officer Robert McLaughlin."

After a moment of silence, Keshen said, "I'm on my way down, I'll be there in a little over an hour."

"I'll be there too."

Before leaving her office, she called Steve Merrill, the Attorney General, and let him know.

****

On the way to the station, Mathews stopped at his house.

"I'll be right back, I need to get something."

After he came out, he got into the car and handed McLaughlin five hundred dollars.

"Here Bobby, take this."

"What's this for?"

"It's for bail or whatever else you need it for."

"I can't take this Rick."

"Take it Bobby, you can pay me back."

Mathews was never paid back.

****

After McLaughlin was in the interview room with Skip Bateman, Mathews went to talk to Bill Wrenn.

"Hi Chief."

"Good work Rick, give me the twenty-five cent recap and then write your report. I contacted Major Sheldon at State Police and they're sending a couple of guys down along with Barbara Keshen"

"I figured State would be handling it and told Bob that. He said that the only person he would talk to is Colon Forbes."

"That works well, because after I called Major Sheldon, Lieutenant Hureau (pronounced hero) called and he's coming down here with Colon and Frank Breen."

"Okay, I'll let Bobby know."

****

Colon Forbes was eating dinner at the Galley Hatch restaurant in Hampton, with his wife and another couple, when his portable bag phone rang. It was a state police phone that was issued to the on call major crimes detective on any given night.

"Hi Colon, it's Mike."

"What's up Mike?"

"I'll meet you at Hampton PD. They have the guy who killed Cushing in custody."

"That's great news, but why are they calling us? I thought they were doing the entire investigation."

"They're calling us because the person who confessed to the murder is Bob McLaughlin."

"Bob McLaughlin the cop?" Colon blurted out and everyone at the table looked at him.

"The same Colon. Evidently, he had a long standing grudge against Cushing and moved in right next to him."

"Holy shit," Forbes said.

Colon's wife knew this was something serious since he rarely swore.

"I'm sorry hon, but I have to go to Hampton PD. They have the person who killed Robert Cushing, and it's one of the Hampton cops."

****

It was ten at night by the time Colon walked out of the interview room with his Walkman tape recorder and spoke to Mike Hureau, Barbara Keshen, Frank Breen, Bill Wrenn and Bob Mark who were in the Chief's conference room.

"He confessed to doing it and gave details. He didn't give me a written statement but I have everything on tape. He also told me that he threw the gun off the route 95 bridge going from Salisbury to Newburyport. I believe it's called the Whittier Bridge."

"Let's make copies of the tape and a transcript as soon as possible," Keshen said.

"We'll get it done first thing tomorrow," Hureau offered.

"Chief Mark, if you don't mind, the press release will come from the AG's office first thing tomorrow."

"That's not a problem, but as soon as it hits the news, we'll be inundated with reporters and TV stations. I'll just refer everything to your office."

"What about McLaughlin's wife Sammi? That's a nickname, her real name is Susan," Forbes asked and then continued, "McLaughlin stated that she did try to stop him but she can possibly be an accessory after the fact."

"I'll look at that tomorrow Keshen said."

"Also, McLaughlin doesn't look well and I think he's a serious suicide risk," Colon said.

"I'll have dispatch get an ambulance here," Wrenn said.

"One more thing," Keshen said. "We need to tell the Cushing's. I think it would best if I did it."

Mark looked at Wrenn who just shrugged. "Okay Barbara, I'm good with that."

****

After the paramedics arrived, they said that Cushing should be in a hospital. His blood pressure and resting heartbeat were off the scale and he was a serious stroke or heart attack risk.

"I'll have some troopers escort the ambulance up and post two troopers in and outside of his room. I'll also let the Major and Colonel know what's going on," Hureau said.

"Thanks Mike," Mark answered.

****

Before Wrenn left, he stopped in at dispatch.

"Fred can you send a general page out to everyone. Tell them we'd like them to make tomorrow's ten AM roll call. Don't tell them about tonight. I'd prefer not to have any leaks."

"Right away chief."

Wrenn then closed his office door and went home. He, like everyone else who was at the PD that night, had a couple of drinks before going to bed.

****

Chief Mark let Keshen use his office to call the Cushings.

"Hello Renny, I'm sorry for the late call, but I have some important information for you."

"That's alright Barbara. What is it?"

"We've arrested the person who killed your father. He confessed tonight and it's Hampton Police Officer Robert McLaughlin. He was off duty that night. We'll be making an announcement tomorrow morning."

It took Renny a moment to process what Keshen had just told him.

"I can't believe it. He's the one who arrested my father and my neighbor Gladys Ring, and we tried to get him fired."

"Well it appears that you were right. Also, and I don't know if you're aware of this, but he lives in the apartment building next to your mom's house."

"He's the one? I knew a cop lived there since we would see the cruiser a lot, but I never knew he was the one."

After a pause, Renny said, "Thanks for the news Barbara, but I need to talk to my family and let them know. Thank you very much."

"And don't worry Renny, we're going to make sure he goes away for a long time."

"I know you will."

Later that night, McLaughlin was transported to the Portsmouth hospital where he stayed for two days under guard from State Troopers. His vitals eventually stabilized and he was then transported to the Rockingham County Prison in Brentwood, NH.

****

When Bill Wrenn got in the next morning at eight, he saw all the detectives were in except for Bill Lally.

Wrenn went to his office and picked up his phone.

"Hey Lall, it's Bill Wrenn."

"Hi Chief."

"I heard you called out."

"Yea, I feel like shit. I hate a summer cold."

"Bill, it's essential you come in. It'll be less than an hour, but you need to be here."

"What's up?"

"I don't want to say over the phone, but you need to be here."

"Okay, I'll be there before 10."

When Bill got to the station he was met by Wrenn in the parking lot.

"You're not going to believe this Lall, but Bob McLaughlin whacked Cushing."

Lally stopped dead in his tracks. "Our Bob McLaughlin?"

"Yea. He confessed last night to Rick Mathews and then Colon Forbes. I suspect most of the guys know by now but I'm making an announcement at roll call."

Lally was stunned.

When he went into roll call, there was none of the banter everyone was accustomed too. It was eerily quiet and one of the guys was trying to hold back tears.

A few minutes later, Bill Wrenn walked in.

"Hello everyone. Without a doubt, this is the most difficult announcement of my life. We've made an arrest on the Cushing case," he paused momentarily to compose himself.

"It's one of our own, Bob McLaughlin."

The police grapevine had been working overtime prior to the announcement and everyone there had heard the rumor. The rumor was confirmed. A few of the guys moaned. Everyone just looked at each other.

To no one's surprise, department moral sank to all-time lows. Half of the department, mainly the newer officers who didn't have a history with McLaughlin, were angry with McLaughlin. How could a cop do this? He not only sullied his name, but that of the department and all cops in general. The other half of the department, McLaughlin's long-time friends, couldn't believe it. He was a model cop who many thought, could handle anything that came his way. They felt it was some sought of mistake, or, he was taking the blame for someone else.

Some remembered the Cushing and Gladys Ring arrests
and how Robert Cushing Sr. and Renny had tried to get him
fired. A few wondered if his wife Sammi had committed
the murders, but many found that implausible since she was
well liked too.

At the moment, it was a lot to take.

****

By eleven AM, Barbara Keshen had made an
announcement to the press that Cushing's murderer was
arrested, and it was Hampton Police Officer, Robert
McLaughlin. She had called for a press conference and the
announcement was made at the Attorney General's office
while she was standing next to Steve Merrill. She told the
reporters that since the investigation was ongoing, there
would be little comment on the particulars of the case. She
did let them know that McLaughlin was currently at the
Portsmouth Hospital under guard because of medical
issues, and the case had been taken over by the NH State
Police. Also if anyone had any info, contact State Police.
As was anticipated, the news was headlined on every
newspaper in the state and the WMUR TV news. It also
was headlined in the Boston papers and 6 PM news. Over
the next week, articles were run daily on Robert
McLaughlin, and after Renny Cushing pointed out that
McLaughlin had taken part in the arrest of his father
thirteen years ago, and that he and his father had tried to get
McLaughlin fired after the arrest of Gladys Ring, it
appeared obvious that this was the result of a long standing
grudge. It also came out that McLaughlin had changed his

name from Randall, and that he had accidently shot his best
friend as a youth, also with a shotgun.

****

Not only was the media camped out around the
Hampton police station, but also in front of Robert
Cushing's house and the apartment building where the
McLaughlin's lived. A number of reporters had rang the
McLaughlin's doorbell and some gained entrance to the
building and knocked on the door. Sammi had the door
locked and didn't answer it. After getting a number of
phone calls by reporters, she unplugged the phone. But not
before calling John Campbell.

"Hi John, this is killing me, first Bob being arrested
and now I have reporters camped out on the road. There
were in the parking lot, but management had them move
off the property."

"Let me see what I can do Sammi. Buzzy Randall
has a place on Hobson Ave that he rents out, but I think it's
empty now."

"That would be great."

Later that day, Campbell, off duty, picked up
Sammi and brought her to the Hobson Ave apartment
which was two blocks from the police department. She
disguised herself as she went out the door and no one
noticed.

****

That night, Beverly McLaughlin Russell, McLaughlin's ex who had remarried, was watching the evening news. She called to her son, "Bob, quick, come watch this." Her son Bob was living with her after moving back from his father's apartment.

The headline news was Cushing's murder and the arrest of her ex-husband. The coverage was extensive.

"Hey Mom," Bob said. Did they say anything about Sammi before I got here?"

"No. Why?"

"Oh nothing, just wondering?"

Beverly looked at her son feeling that he knew something he wasn't telling her.

Several days later, at the dinner table, Bob Jr, turned towards his mother and said, "Mom, there's something I need to tell you."

****

Once again, John Tommasi was on the farmer's porch of 16 M street drinking coffee and reading the morning paper. Fred Rheault was there too.

"Fredso, you're not going to believe this."

"Not going to believe what."

Remember that murder that happened at the beginning of summer here in Hampton?"

"Yea, it happened somewhere uptown."

"Yea, Bob McLaughlin just confessed to it and he's being held at Brentwood county jail.

"Bob McLaughlin, the Hampton cop who's been here a few times having beers."

"Yea, that one."

"No shit."

"Huh, I didn't see that one coming."

"No shit."

****

Paul Cronin was the Chief of Police in Seabrook when he received a call from Beverly Russell. Cronin knew Russell since the early seventies when he started his police career at Hampton as a part-time police officer, and he knew she and Bob McLaughlin had been divorced. He received a job offer at Seabrook as a full time officer and rose through the ranks before becoming Chief.

"Hi Beverly, what can I do for you. "

"I'm sure you've heard of Bob's arrest."

"I have."

"Well my son has some information for you. In July, both Bob and his wife told Bob junior that senior killed Cushing and Sammi planned the whole thing."

"Is junior willing to give me a statement?"

"Yes he is."

"I'll be right there."

Before he left, he called Bob Mark and advised him of the phone call he received.

"Thanks Paul, I'll let Colon Forbes know, he and Mike are working out of Hampton. Let Junior know that Colon will probably want to talk to him."

"Yea, I figured as much. I'll do a report and then get it right over to you."

****

Chief Cronin found that Bob junior's memory was extremely lucid and he incriminated Sammi McLaughlin as an accomplice to murder. He somewhat incriminated himself as an accomplice after the fact by knowing about the murder and not contacting the police, but he was relatively sure that in exchange for testifying, he would receive immunity.

By the time he went back to the PD and typed out the report, it was close to eleven in the morning. He then called Bob Mark.

"Hi Bob, is now a good time to come over? It seems that Sammi McLaughlin planned the murder and was a lookout when McLaughlin shot Cushing."

"Yea, Colon is here too. I'll let him know you're on your way."

"Be there in fifteen."

****

When Cronin entered Hampton PD, he was recognized and admitted right away. He went to Chief Mark's office. Bill Wrenn and Colon Forbes were also there.

After greetings were exchanged Cronin gave everyone copies he had made of his report.

"Here's the Cliff Notes version. Bob junior not only confirmed senior's confession to Mathews and Colon, he implicated McLaughlin's wife as an accomplice. He told me that when he went to his dad's apartment, Sammi wasn't there and after a while, senior told junior that he committed the murder almost exactly the way senior confessed. After senior told him, Sammi came home and he let her know that he told junior. She was upset at first, but after he assured her that his son could be trusted, she open up to him and told junior how she had planned the whole thing, disguising herself as a young man, Bob wearing black, parking the truck on presidential drive and walking over to Cushing's and then throwing the gun off the route 95 bridge that goes over the Merrimac river."

"Will he talk to us?" Colon asked.

"Yea he will. He doesn't think he's in any trouble, but I'm sure he'll cooperate, and here's his number. He's staying at his mother's house and he's just working part-time."

"That's good. I'll call him now," Colon said.

"One other thing," Wrenn said. "Let's keep this close to our chest. Sammi has a lot of friends here in the department. I'm sure no one would compromise the investigation, but let's not take any chances."

Everyone nodded their heads.

Colon went back to the office he was given at the PD and called junior. He agreed to come to the PD the next day at 10 AM and talk to Colon. It would be the first day of September and he finally got a break after searching five days for the description of the person given by Mary Cheney. He then got on the phone with Barbara Keshen.

Chapter 8
The Investigation, September

Bob junior came to the station the next day accompanied by his mother. Colon was waiting for them in the lobby along with Barbara Keshen. After introductions were made, Colon showed them to his office.

"Trooper Forbes, I'd like to know if my son is in trouble."

"No he is not. That's why Barbara Keshen is here."

"Here's an agreement I have if you'd like to read it over and I'm also authorized to sign it and give Bob that immunity. Please realize, if he lies to us, he will be in trouble," Keshen said.

"This isn't a problem," Bob answered and after he and his mother read it, he signed it. He then told Colon the same story he told Paul Cronin the day before. Both Keshen and Forbes liked it, because if someone is retelling a story that is false, there are usually discrepancies. Forbes had his recorder out and recorded the entire interview.

After a moment's thought, Colon asked, "Bob, we'd like to get her to admit it on tape. Would you be willing to call her on the phone and try to get her to say that again?"

"Sure, I can do that."

"Okay Bob, we'll be in touch. Is there anything else you or your mom have any questions on?" Forbes asked.

"No, I think we're all set," Beverly answered after looking at her son.

After Colon walked Beverly and Bob junior out of the station, he went back to his office where Keshen was writing notes.

"Colon, what do you think of getting a wiretap on Sammi McLaughlin's phone. I heard she moved to a summer cottage by the PD."

"Yea, she's two blocks down the road. One of the Hampton cops owns it and she's staying there. She's also retained a lawyer, Bruce Kenna out of Manchester."

"Bruce is a good defense lawyer," Keshen stated.

"I've heard. I'll get to work on the search warrant and we'll run it pass Judge Frazier tomorrow."

Judge Whitey Frazier was the well-respected Hampton District Court's judge. He was tough on crime but demanded excellence from his officers.

"Alright, I'll contact him and let him know it's coming. I'll be here first thing in the AM to take a look at it."

"Sounds good Barbara. I'll have it done by then."

****

After lunch the next day, Forbes and Keshen were shown into Judge Frazier's chambers. Colon had been before Judge Frazier in the past and there was a mutual respect. It was the first time for Keshen. Pleasantries were exchanged and Frazier invited them to have a seat.

"That's terrible about Bob McLaughlin, I always liked him," Frazier said.

"I know judge. I spoke to him a month ago at Handy Dan's. We had coffee and he was looking forward to retirement. It came as a surprise." Keshen said nothing.

"So what do you have Colon?"

"It's a search warrant for a wiretap on McLaughlin's wife's phone. We have very credible information, in the form of a statement from Bob McLaughlin's son that Sammi confessed to him in planning the whole thing, and then stood as lookout. Sammi is her nickname, her real name is Susan."

With that, Judge Frazier began to read the affidavit to the search warrant for the wiretap, which was five pages long.

"As usual Colon, it's very complete and conclusive, but I have one problem."

"What's that judge?"

"I've heard that Mrs. McLaughlin has retained counsel. Any calls between her and her lawyer are privileged and confidential, and not subject to this warrant. I'm going to sign with that proviso. Attorney Keshen, I will hold you responsible for the state to make sure this is upheld."

"Judge, you can rest assured that will never happen," Keshen answered.

With that, Judge Frazier signed the warrant and Forbes and Keshen left.

When they got back to the PD, Colon called Mike Hureau and advised him they had the wiretap.

"That's good. I'll get the techies to install it. They're expecting my call," Mike said.

"Excellent."

The wiretap was up and running the next day and manned by State Troopers around the clock. They had strict instructions to turn it, and the tape recorder off if she had conversations with her attorney.

****

The next day, Keshen called Forbes from her office in Concord. He was still working out of Hampton PD.

"Colon, when do you want to have McLaughlin's son call the wife?"

"I want to wait sometime. If they talk together on the phone, I want to see if he says anything that is different from his story to us or maybe she will incriminate herself more to him. Before the arrest of Bob senior, junior thought he and Sammi were getting along well."

"Let me know what you get."

"You'll be the first."

"One other thing, Colon, I was contacted by her lawyer, Bruce Kenna, we are not to talk to Sammi without him present."

"I'm not surprised, Kenna is every bit as good as Mark Sisti, Bob's lawyer."

"He is. Talk to you soon."

On Wednesday, September 7th, Sammi called Bob junior.

****

After the phone call was transcribed and a duplicate tape made, Forbes called Keshen.

"Hi Barbara."

"Hi Colon, what do you have?'

"We have Sammi calling Bob junior to wish him happy birthday. Seems like everyone forgot about it. It was a pretty benign phone call where they talked about Bob senior most of the time and the upcoming grand jury for Bob senior starting next Monday the 12th. The only good part of the conversation was her telling junior not to say anything that she or his dad told him. So we got her on witness tampering too."

"That's great. Anything else?"

"No that's it."

"Alright, and just to let you know, another assistant AG, Steve Winer, will be helping me on the case."

"I know Steve, good man. Tell him I said hi."

"I will."

****

When Colon arrived at Hampton PD, Tuesday, September 13, there was a message waiting for him from Beverly Russell, Bob senior's ex. She had called the night before and she was scheduled to testify at Bob's grand jury hearing that was in its second day. He hoped to get her before she left the house.

"Hi Beverly, it's Colon Forbes."

"Hi Colon, I was about to leave for court. I got a call from Sammi last night. That bitch threatened me and said she would get me if I said anything bad about Bob in court."

"Bev, can you come in and make a statement?" The grand jury is expected to go on for a couple of more days. I can call Barbara Keshen at the court and have you rescheduled for tomorrow?"

"That's good Colon. I'll be leaving shortly."

Colon then called the Rockingham County Superior Court, identified himself, and asked for Barbara Keshen. She answered within five minutes.

"Yes Colon."

"Can you reschedule Beverly Russell for tomorrow? She just called me and she was threatened by Sammi McLaughlin last night via phone. We don't have that on the tape, so she must have called from somewhere else."

"That won't be a problem. But it would've been nice to have that on tape," Keshen said

"Let's do this Barbara, Bob junior is testifying this morning, right?"

"Yes he is."

"Why don't we have him come in today after he testifies and call Sammi from the PD and tell her that he didn't appreciate his mom being threatened? I'm sure we'll get Sammi incriminating herself. Not only that, but we can have him tell her that he testified to the grand jury today and told them all about her."

"Great idea. Let me know what happens."

Bob junior came in that afternoon at 5PM after testifying and called Sammi McLaughlin.

****

After hellos were exchanged, Sammi said, "I saw your uncle Maurice at court today."

"Did he tell you anything?"

"No why?"

"Because I was subpoenaed to grand jury and testified today."

"Did you go?"

"Yea I had to, and my uncle didn't tell you anything."

"No why," Sammi asked again.

"The news."

"What news?"

"What I told the state police."

"What did you tell them Bobby?"

"I told them everything that you and Dad confessed to me."

"Why?"

"Because it was the right thing to do because my father's already in prison and you're out walking around and you helped him and I feel you oughta go to jail for it too."

"Well I can appreciate your honesty Bobby, very much, but nobody's approached me on it."

"They haven't questioned you on it yet?"

"No."

"I'm stunned they haven't because I told them everything I know."

"Well what can I say Bobby."

"You don't have anything really to say to me, huh?"

"No. I mean what can I say? You know, things happen in life."

"I figured that after I told you and stuff, you were going to threaten me like you did my mom."

"Well I just didn't know what she was going to say when I told her I would get her. I was doing it for your dad Bobby. I didn't want her to say anything that would incriminate your dad."

"Well, what I said is going to incriminate the both of you."

"It may not. I don't know. I guess I got to call my lawyer and tell him."

"I'm surprised that you haven't told me that you hated me or anything."

"No I don't hate you. I really don't. Take care of yourself and keep your chin up."

"Okay."

"Bye, bye Bobby."

"Bye."

Author's note: The above is a close to exact transcription from the written record of the wiretap.

****

The following day, Colon Forbes obtained an arrest warrant for Sammi McLaughlin. She was arrested at 3 PM, transported to Rockingham County Jail in Brentwood for booking, and then transferred to Merrimack County Jail, since Rockingham had limited facilities for females. She was held without bail.

At her arraignment the next day, she plead not guilty to the charges of: conspiracy to commit murder, accomplice to murder, and two counts of witness tampering. The following day there was a bail hearing where her lawyer, Bruce Kenna, asked that she be released on PR bail given her spotless prior record. PR bail was denied by the judge, but he did set a bail of $10,000 which Sammi was able to produce since Bob McLaughlin had cashed in his police retirement account. She remained out on bail until she was found guilty at trial the following year.

****

The day after his arrest, Bob McLaughlin was appointed a public defender who asked that he be released on bail. It was denied and he was held without bail. The following day, he was charged with first degree murder which, in New Hampshire at the time, carried the death penalty or life without parole. Barbara Keshen, who was adamantly against the death penalty, wanted to seek life without parole. However, before she made this public, she had to get Steve Merrill's consent, and although she didn't need to, she wanted to make sure it was alright with the Cushing family.

She wasn't too surprised to find that Renny Cushing and the rest of the family were against the death penalty also, especially Renny. After relaying this to Steve Merrill, he acquiesced and she proceeded to prosecute, seeking a sentence of life without parole.

****

The press was learning more and more about McLaughlin's past life. The AG's office played their cards very close to their chest and said very little since "the investigation was ongoing." The papers continued to dig, and on September 2, they published an article where they interviewed a neighbor of the Cushings, Ann Johnson, who was on the scene of the double fatal on Winnacunnet road the night Cushing was arrested in 1975. She stated, "There was gas all over the road and the police told Bob Cushing to put out the cigarette. They said 'you'll blow us up if you don't put out that cigarette.' He didn't and after they asked him a second time, he was arrested and marched down to the paddy wagon."

Keshen did not comment on this arrest or the arrest of Gladys Ring the month after Cushing was arrested.

The papers also interviewed many of McLaughlin's co-workers at the police department who to a person, described McLaughlin as a model, spit and polish cop. This was echoed by Skip Sullivan, the fire chief and other members of the community. The building manager who rented McLaughlin the apartment at Elsie Gardens described him as a model tenant who was always friendly and paid the rent on time. She also liked the fact that there was a police officer living in the apartments.

Doctor Seemans was contacted but he refused to comment on any aspect of the case.

By early September, McLaughlin had hired Mark Sisti and his law firm of Sisti and Twomey. He was able to pay Sisti by cashing in his police retirement pension.

Mark Sisti, by many, was viewed as the best defense attorney in the state. He later defended Pam Smart.

Mark obtained his B.A. from Canisius College in 1976 and his J.D. from UNH Law in 1979. He started his career as a public defender in New Hampshire, and was the Deputy Director of the NH Public Defenders office from 1985 through 1988. He went into private practice in early 1988.

Author' note: both now and then, if a police officer is convicted of a felony before he takes his pension, he/she forfeits that pension. However since McLaughlin was not convicted, he was still entitled to it. The pension system was recently changed to 30 years of service and reaching age 55 for a full pension from 20 years and age 45.

****

By September 5th, Sisti had achieved a number of milestones motions. The Grand Jury hearing was scheduled to begin September 12th and expected to last the week.

First and foremost, he recanted McLaughlin's confession. In a motion to suppress, Sisti's motion stated that on the night of the murder, McLaughlin was suffering from a "severe psychiatric condition" complicated by ingesting huge amounts of alcohol and prescription drugs. McLaughlin was in a confused rambling mental state aggravated by exceptionally high blood pressure.

Sisti also took the unusual step of petitioning the court in order to present evidence at the grand jury that would be favorable to his client.

The grand jury usually follows a probable cause hearing by a judge. The probable cause hearing determines if there was sufficient evidence for an arrest. This occurred in August with McLaughlin at the Hampton District Court.

If the judge finds "probable cause" the case will be sent to the Grand Jury. The Grand Jury is a panel of between 12 and 23 persons who determine whether there is enough evidence to "indict" (formally charge) the defendant. Generally at a grand jury hearing, neither the defendant nor his/her lawyer is present.

Both of Sisti's motions were rejected in Superior Court and a subsequent "True Bill" was found by the grand jury.

Author's note: a true bill is the written decision of the Grand Jury (signed by the Grand Jury foreperson) that it has heard sufficient evidence from the prosecution to believe that an accused person probably committed a crime and should be indicted and bound for trial.

The Court appointed Judge was the Honorable Robert H. Temple who was then assigned to the Strafford County Superior Court. It is not uncommon in New Hampshire for a judge from another county to preside over a high profile trial in an adjacent county.

Judge Temple was born 7/28/27 in Coronado, CA. the son of Harry and Blanch Temple. Judge Temple graduated from Nashua High School, Boston University and then the Boston University School of Law. Judge Temple was an accomplished trial lawyer with the law firm of Fisher, Parsons, Moran and Temple in Dover for 20 years. He was appointed as a Superior Court Judge by Governor Gallen in 1979, and he presided over the Strafford County Superior Court until his retirement in 1995.

****

In early September, prior to the arrest of Sammi McLaughlin, Bill Lally called for a meeting of the Hampton Police Union to discuss what they should do for Bob McLaughlin, if anything. Bill was the Union President. The meeting was held in the training room of the old Hampton Fire Station. Moral was low and the union was split on what to do. At times the meeting was contentious. It was finally decided that the Bob McLaughlin defense fund would be started which would include donations and the raffling of a Harley Davidson Motorcycle. There were many, at the time, who believed that McLaughlin didn't do it and he was covering for someone else, possible, his wife. They were able to raise $5000.

Tim Collins had left the meeting early and as he was leaving, he noticed a white full sized van. He knew that State Police had a surveillance van similar to that and wondered if the union meeting was being monitored. State Police has never confirmed or denied this.

****

Since the arrest of Bob McLaughlin there was always concern about not having the murder weapon. However, the concentration of the State Police investigators was focused on the arrest of Sammi McLaughlin and the subsequent grand jury hearing. Towards the end of September, Barbara Keshen called Lt Hureau.

"Hi Lieutenant, it's Barbara Keshen."

"Hello Barbara, what can I do for you?"

"Has any progress been made on locating the murder weapon."

"Colon and I have been talking about it. Bob McLaughlin told Colon that he threw the shotgun off the bridge over the Merrimac River between Salisbury and Newburyport the night Cushing was murdered. We've been in touch with Tim McClaire of Fish & Game. He's the head of their search & rescue team. He's trying to get some divers together for a search."

"That's great. Keep me in the loop."

"I will."

****

It was October 7th by the time Tim McClaire was able to assemble his team. He decided there would be two teams of two divers that would alternate diving from their Fish & Game boat which was slipped in Portsmouth. By the time they cleared the Piscataqua River, the wind kicked up and they were encountering 4-6 foot waves which forced them to turn back. The forecast for the next day was the same, and as a result, they trailered the boat and brought it down to the Golden Anchor Marina on the Merrimac to launch it.

They timed the dive to be two hours before and after slack tide since the rivers current was significant. They were also assisted by the Salisbury and Newburyport harbor Masters on their boats who diverted river traffic around the divers. The Fish and Game boat stayed above the divers while displaying a dive flag.

Because of his status as a police officer, he was not searched like other visitors. In a couple of minutes, McLaughlin, in an orange jumpsuit, was led to the partition and picked up the phone. Lally did the same since this was the way that visitors spoke to prisoners.

"How ya doin' Bobby?"

"I'm doing good Lall. Thanks for coming."

"You feeling better."

"Yea I am. I'm on some medication so my blood pressure is down. But being here really sucks. I'm on some happy drugs too, so my anxiety is down."

"That's good Bobby. I hear you got Sisti and Twomey as lawyers."

"Yea I did. I had to cash in my retirement to pay them, but they're the best."

"That's good Bobby. Lot of the guys are behind you and we're doing a raffle for ya. We're getting a Harley and selling tickets for $100 each."

"Thanks Lall, tell the other guys I said thanks."

Small talk continued for another fifteen minutes before Lally said he had to go.

Just before he got up, McLaughlin said one last thing.

"Lall, I have to tell you, I didn't do it."

Bill just nodded his head and waved before he left.

Chapter 9
The Susan McLaughlin Trial
April, 1989

Bruce Kenna shared a status similar to Mark Sisti as a defense lawyer. Bruce was a graduate of Colgate University, (where he was a member of the varsity wrestling team) and Albany Law School at Union University. He was admitted to the NH bar in 1976. Like Sisti, he started his career in the NH Public Defender's office and eventually became the director of that office. By 1988, he had his own private practice and was a prominent defense lawyer.

The jury, consisting of 9 men and 3 women, was picked in March. The trial began on Monday, April 10, 1989. Judge Robert Temple was presiding.

One of the first questions that many people had, was why was the Sammi McLaughlin trial for accessory to murder before the murder trial of Bob McLaughlin?

The simple fact of the matter was that the cases were being handled as separate trials. The AG's office did not make an issue of the Sammi McLaughlin trial going first and neither defense attorneys objected. Bob McLaughlin's trial was scheduled for Mid-May of 1989.

The next question that many had was what happens if Robert McLaughlin is found not guilty of murder? Will his wife's sentence then be commuted if she was found guilty? The answer to that question is most likely no as a result of legal case precedent.

James Duggan, a Law Professor at Franklin Pierce Law Center in Concord, NH was interviewed and he cited the case of Kathy Kaplan who plead guilty in 1982 to hiring an assassin to kill her allegedly abusive husband. She made her plea with the understanding she would testify against the gunman who was eventually acquitted, but the gunman was found not guilty. Her conviction was appealed by her lawyer on the grounds that she couldn't be an accomplice to an accused defendant who was found not guilty. Her appeal was denied, however, her sentence was reduced in 1987 by then Governor John Sunnunu.

Keshen stated that she was not familiar with the Kaplan case and did not comment as to whether the cases were similar. As it turned out, it wasn't a concern. *Authors note: Most of the above is paraphrased from an article in the Hampton Union Newspaper.*

****

Assisting Barbara Keshen for the prosecution was Mike Ramsdell, another assistant AG. Michael received his BA from Central Connecticut State University and his JD from New York law school. After passing the NH bar, he started his law career as a clerk to a federal judge. He was then hired by Steve Merrill as an assistant AG and after a number of successful trials where his talent was evident, he was made head of the homicide unit. In addition, Michael served as Associate Attorney General for the Division of Public Protection, which includes the Criminal Justice Bureau, the Consumer Protection Bureau, and the Environmental Protection Bureau.

After leaving the AG's office, he joined the law firm of Sheehan & Phinney, located in Manchester, Concord and Boston.

The opening statements consisted of Mike Ramsdell recounting the events of June 1, 1988 and the subsequent confession of Robert McLaughlin Sr. to his son in late July. He also stated that there would be taped conversations of Sammi McLaughlin to Bob McLaughlin Jr. and evidence of witness tampering.

Bruce Kenna's opening statement began by countering that Robert McLaughlin Jr. was an unreliable witness, with a history of mental illness and substance abuse. He also pointed out the discrepancy of witness's description of a young white male leaving the murder scene and how that was clearly not Susan McLaughlin. He ended his statement by saying, "It's going to be an interesting trial; I hope you enjoy it."

Court was then adjourned and the 12 members of the jury, and 3 alternates toured the scene of the Elsie Garden apartments, in addition to the front door and entrance way of the Cushing home and the backyard. Witnesses were to be called the next day. Also present during the entire trial was either Mark Sisti or Paul Twomey.

****

The first witness was Marie Cushing. The defense argued that her appearance as a witness was not necessary because the defense was not contesting the facts of death. The prosecution argued that it was essential that Marie

Cushing testify to lay a foundation and portray the callousness of the murder. Judge Temple agreed with the prosecution.

Marie Cushing testified how she was watching the Celtics game and how Robert Cushing answered the door after a knock. She continued and described how she saw the red flare of the gun and how her husband's body was thrown into the air and backwards. She then recounted how she remembered screaming and how it took a while before she was able to call the police station.

Kenna declined any cross examination and Marie quickly left the court room accompanied by some of her children.

The next witnesses were John Smith and his daughter Linda, the Cushing's neighbors. They testified how they heard the shots and thought they were fireworks. Linda also testified to seeing two people run from the Cushing's house.

When she was cross examined by attorney Kenna, Linda couldn't identify Sammi McLaughlin as one of the persons who was running away from the Cushing house towards Presidential Circle.

On redirect, Michael Ramsdell asked if Sammi McLaughlin roughly fit the height and weight description of the person she saw, which she confirmed.

Mary Cheney, who was driving home from shopping was also called to the stand and she testified how she saw a person who she thought was a young man with slicked backed brown hair.

The results were pretty much the same as Linda Smith. She couldn't positively identify Sammi as that person, but she could confirm the person she saw was approximately the same height and build as Sammi McLaughlin.

The last witness of the day for the prosecution, was Dr. Roger Fossum, the state medical examiner who performed the autopsy on Richard Cushing.

Fossum's testimony was an in depth account of the manner in which Cushing died and the damage that two large shotgun slugs are capable of doing when fired at close range to an individual's abdomen.

Kenna had no questions for Fossum who was subsequently excused and court was adjourned for the day.

****

The next day experienced a twist. An evidentiary hearing was scheduled where the jurors were not to be present. Judge Temple also ruled that the press would not be allowed to report on the proceedings. This was immediately appealed to the NH Supreme court by the Union Leader (the largest paper by circulation in the state) and the Court agreed to hear it immediately and issue a decision. The hearing was put off until the Supreme Court heard arguments from the paper which was the next day. The court's decision came on the same day as the hearing.

The state Supreme Court ruled that the press could be present, and the hearing was scheduled for the following day, April 17.

****

The entire day consisted of the evidentiary hearing of Sergeant Rick Mathews. The purpose of the hearing was to determine the admissibility of evidence and whether its presentation will compromise the fairness of a trial. During this hearing, the jury was not present but the press was.

Mathews began his testimony by recounting how long he had known McLaughlin and how they were best friends. He was also one of the few people who knew the stress that McLaughlin was enduring and his heavy drinking when he wasn't on duty. Upon further questioning by Ramsdell, Mathews also revealed that he knew that Bob McLaughlin had been under psychiatric care and had been on psychiatric leave in 1986. Mathews, however, very emphatically stated that McLaughlin never drank on duty, was a model policeman who was always impeccably dressed and was a real "cops cop."

Mathews also recalled some "gallows humor" on how some cops during roll call or in the locker room had kiddingly accused McLaughlin of killing Robert Cushing because Cushing had tried to get him fired in the mid 1970's.

Lastly, Mathews testified how McLaughlin had confessed to him on August 26, 1988. He began by stating that Sammi McLaughlin had told him how she tried to stop her husband from killing his neighbor but he had brushed her aside. Mathews also said that this was corroborated by Bob McLaughlin. During the ride to Pease Air Force base to see the psychiatrist, McLaughlin had kept up a rambling conversation on a number of subjects, however, McLaughlin caught Mathews's ear when he said that he was watching the movie Apocalypse Now before the killing. Mathews said that McLaughlin quoted a line from the movie on how the central character in the movie stated that, "The only way good can overcome evil, is to become more evil."

Mathews then recounted that McLaughlin told him that he dressed in black in preparation for the killing, parked his car down the road at presidential circle, ran to Cushing's house, knocked on the front door and shot him twice with his shotgun through the screen door.

In cross examination by the defense, Bruce Kenna, Mathews also testified that some of his superiors were aware of the animosity McLaughlin held towards Cushing and knew that he was under psychiatric care. Lastly, Mathews testified that he was aware of an allegation by Robert McLaughlin Jr. that he, Mathews, had tried to provide an alibi for Sammi McLaughlin while her husband killed Cushing. Mathews stated that those allegations "were not true."

The purpose of that question by Bruce Kenna was to discredit the story of Robert McLaughlin Jr. who was scheduled to testify after Mathews once the trial was resumed.

Judge Temple ruled that the Mathews's testimony could be heard in open court.

Authors note: there was absolutely no evidence that Sergeant Mathews tried to provide Sammi McLaughlin with an alibi. Quite the contrary, McLaughlin would not have been brought to justice if not for Mathews.

****

The next day began with the testimony of Rick Mathews and went exactly as it had during the evidentiary hearing with no surprises.

The next to testify was Robert McLaughlin Jr.

AG Ramsdell ask McLaughlin to describe the relationship he had with his father and stepmother.

He said that he didn't have the typical father-son relationship with his father. It was a minimal relationship during his teen years but it took a turn for the worse when his father divorced his mother Beverly when he was sixteen. He resented his father for a number of reasons but particularly since he had to quit school to help support his mother and two sisters.

He went on to state that when he was twenty-one, he began to see his father again and was introduced to Sammi. He got along well with Sammi and his relationship with his father began to improve to the point where he started visiting his father at the Elsie Garden Apartments. They also began to take karate classes together with Bob senior paying for junior's classes. However, at some point, the relationship was severed for reasons that he didn't expound upon (quite possibly Bob juniors drug use and rehab).

He then visited his father in July of 1988 to reopen the relationship after his father called. The visit was a pleasant surprise to his father and he invited him in to talk after they embraced.

"Sammi was out doing errands at the time," McLaughlin Jr. testified

At first, junior said, the conversation touched on "typical things" while his father sat down drinking a beer with vodka shooters. But at some point, his father had something he really wanted to tell him and repeated it a number of times.

After a period of silence, his father said "that he had shot and killed someone."

"What did you think of this?" Ramsdell asked.

"At first I thought the shooting was related to police work. I knew that he had previously been in a couple of gunfights. My dad then said no, it had nothing to do with police work but he could get into a lot of trouble for it."

McLaughlin junior then related how his father had told him of the events thirteen years earlier when he arrested Robert Cushing and then Gladys Ring and how Robert and Renny Cushing tried to get him and Rick Mathews fired. He also told junior that Sammi was the one who planned it so he wouldn't get caught and said that her plan was better.

"What happened next?" Ramsdell asked.

"Well in about ten to fifteen minutes Sammi came home and when my dad told her that he told me about the killing, her jaw dropped. She just looked at my dad and said that we weren't supposed to tell anyone. My dad then assured her that I wouldn't tell anyone and that I could be trusted."

Bob junior then recounted how Sammi then opened up to him and reaffirmed what his father told him.

McLaughlin then testified that his stepmother told me "That he (McLaughlin Sr.) had to have a better idea and that he couldn't go out and just do it. My stepmother then told me that she had waited outside the Cushing house with her karate staff in case anyone happened to come by."

McLaughlin also testified that his stepmother was about to reveal the location of the murder weapon but was stopped by his father. After he finished a beer that his father gave him, he left the apartment for the night.

"Did anything else happen?" Ramsdell asked.

"Yes, the following day my Dad came to visit me in Seabrook and said it would be best if I forgot about the conversation."

"No further questions."

****

After a brief recess, Bruce Kenna began his cross examination, and he concentrated on questioning the credibility and believability of McLaughlin's testimony and his character.

Kenna started with some inconsistencies in McLaughlin's reports to police. These questions were answered primarily by "I don't remember."

Kenna next concentrated on McLaughlin's episodes of drug abuse and his admittance to Portsmouth hospital. Kenna also questioned McLaughlin on his treatment by Seacoast Mental Health for a number of different psychosis.

"You were acting pretty bizarre weren't you, including washing your hands more than one hundred times per day?" Kenna said.

"I was washing my hands a lot but I don't think it was that much and that stopped way before I got back with my father in July when he confessed."

"Didn't you also say that other people were controlling your thoughts?"

"No, I don't remember ever saying that. People influenced me, but never controlled me."

Kenna continued, "Mr. McLaughlin, why doesn't this allegation about your stepmother come to light in any of the investigative reports until after you tell your mother?" Kenna asked.

"I'm not sure. I guess I wanted to protect my stepmother, but then I thought it wasn't fair my father should take the entire blame."

Kenna had no further questions.

Ramsdell's redirect concentrated on the fact that McLaughlin Jr. was not using drugs at the time of his father's admission or under any psychiatric care.
Authors note: Even though psychology is far from an exact science, most pyschologists will agree that compulsive hand washing is indicative of an attempt to relieve stress as a result of feelings of guilt such as Lady MacBeth in Hamlet.

****

The following day, the jurors listened to the two recorded conversations between Sammi McLaughlin and Robert McLaughlin Jr. Ramsdell explained to the jury that the tapes provided ample evidence for witness tampering. Specifically, when Sammi told Junior not to tell the Grand Jury anything and that she would do anything to protect her husband. There was also talk as to Sammi McLaughlin's call to Senior's divorced wife and how Sammi told Beverly the same thing. McLaughlin Jr. had previously testified that he was not coached about what topics to bring up or what to say while speaking with his stepmother.

Kenna pointed out to the jury that while evidence may exist on the tape of jury tampering, there was absolutely nothing on the tapes that implicated Sammi McLaughlin as an accomplice to murder.

****

Mike Ramsdell and Barbara Keshen were in a private room at Rockingham Court house reserved for the prosecution.

"What do you think Mike."

"Kenna made a good point. While I think we have no problem getting a guilty finding on witness tampering, there was nothing on the tapes implicating her as an accomplice the night of the murder."

"I agree," Keshen said. "The only thing we have is the testimony of Bob Junior and some circumstantial evidence indicating that Sammi matches the weight and height of the person the two witnesses saw that night."

"I think that should be enough. Keep in mind, Sammi didn't deny anything on the tapes when junior said his father was in prison and it's not fair that she's not either."

"I hope so."

****

The following day, Beverly Russell, McLaughlin's ex-wife, and Stephanie Ross a former Hampton Police Dispatcher, were called to the stand.

Russell testified that after her son told her of her ex's confession to him, she called Chief Cronin to come and interview Bob junior which he did. She also testified that she called her ex's sister, Ivy Blanchard. She said she told Blanchard about the confession and how her ex-husband had already given himself up to police investigators, and how her son was going to tell police about Sammi's involvement.

"Ivy said we were going to hang him," said Russell.

Russell then testified that the next day, Sammi McLaughlin called her and said, "If you hurt my Bobby, you'll pay. If he's convicted, I'll get you sooner or later."

On cross examination, Kenna was able to get Russell to admit that she "hated Robert McLaughlin for what he did to me and my children" and at one time contemplated shooting him with his own revolver.

The last witness for the prosecution was Stephanie Ross, the ex-dispatcher from Hampton, PD. Ross told the court that she was a friend of the McLaughlin's since she was a teenager and turned to the couple for advice after a "very confusing" childhood which included a lot of trauma. They were still friends when Robert McLaughlin was arrested and she tried to be a resource to Sammi. When she went to see Sammi one day in September, Sammi told her that she called Beverly Russell in a "fit of inebriated indignation" and told her not to testify. But the people who were in the hotel room where she made the call, would swear that she did not make the call.

When it came time for Bruce Kenna to cross-examine Ross, Ross testified that Sammi had told her to be truthful if she went before the grand jury but not to volunteer anything.

Ross also admitted under cross-examination that on September 6, she lied to a State Trooper when she said that she didn't know anything about the murder even though she had visited McLaughlin in the hospital after he was arrested and he had confessed to her.

Ross stated, "I was afraid to hurt Bobby or Sammi. That's why I lied to the Trooper."

"No further questions," Kenna said.

"Your honor, the state rests," Ramsdell replied without any redirect questions for Ross.

****

Kenna's first witness was Robert McLaughlin Sr.'s sister, Ivy Blanchard. She testified that she and her husband visited Sammi McLaughlin the night that Sammi called from her (Ivy) hotel room and allegedly threatened Beverly Russell. She stated, "Knowing Beverly the way I do, I just know they were lies. She hates my brother and Sammi, and Beverly would do anything to hurt them." She also stated that when she was leaving, Sammi was going to bed. There was no record of the phone call since on a landline, Hampton to Seabrook is a local call.

Kenna's next witnesses were several State Troopers who simply testified that they were stationed outside of McLaughlin's room at the Portsmouth hospital and they were there to guard him and make sure he didn't commit suicide.

The last witness for the defense was Chief Paul Cronin of Seabrook.

After he was contacted by Beverly Russell, who he knew, he spoke to her briefly over the phone to ascertain what information that her son had. Before going to the Russell house, Cronin testified that he called Barbara Keshen who said not to advise McLaughlin Jr. of his rights to self-incrimination and to take an initial statement, and state investigators would conduct a more complete interview. Cronin also stated that he took abbreviated notes while he was interviewing McLaughlin Jr.

"Were those notes you took complete, or did you leave some parts out of Robert McLaughlin junior's statement?" Kenna asked.

Cronin replied that was not the case. Cronin then testified that McLaughlin Jr. clearly implicated Senior in the murder and Sammi in the planning and as an accomplice since that was what they confessed to him.

Cronin also denied that his notes reflected any attempt to obscure the statement that he was recording.

Bruce Kenna did not get what he was hoping, however he felt that any doubt that was planted in the minds of jurors was significant.

The Defense rested and Judge Temple adjourned for the day. The next day, April 28th, would be the closing arguments to the jury.

****

After ten days of trial, the jury heard closing arguments. During the closing arguments, defense is given much leeway and generally, the state cannot object. If the defense attorney says something that is incorrect or particularly egregious, the judge may intercede.

Defense Attorney Bruce Kenna spoke first and began by describing the brutal murder of Robert Cushing Sr. by two shotgun blasts.

Defenses plan was to indicate that testimony from nearly all of the states fifteen witnesses did not directly implicate Sammi McLaughlin.

Kenna argued that, "As a result of the description of every witness that came forward the night of the murder and the next day, police were seeking a young white male."

Kenna then went on to say that when questioned by three police officers about her role in the murder, Sammi McLaughlin stated she had tried to stop her husband, including trying to physically restrain him by using a karate staff, but to no avail.

Kenna then changed tacks and addressed the most damning testimony, that of Robert McLaughlin Jr. He stated that it was not until after the arrest of Robert McLaughlin Sr. did the son come forward and implicate his stepmother. "He could have easily fabricated the story in the wake of newspaper reports. Bobby Junior has plenty of reason to lie to authorities in order to exact retribution on his father by divorcing his mother and abandoning the family, thereby forcing him to quit school and go to work to help support the his mother and two younger sisters as a teenager."

Kenna then attacked McLaughlin's character. He emphasized to the jury that you have to examine the witness's credibility. "You have to look at their demeanor in the courtroom, the evidence presented and whether the witness has cause to obscure the truth."

Kenna pointed out the younger McLaughlin's drug abuse, psychiatric care and "bizarre behavior."

"This guy, (Robert McLaughlin Jr.) has real deep-seated problems in numerous reports, including how his doctors spoke of his 'quiet rage'. Doctors have also noted that Robert McLaughlin Jr. has trouble distinguishing between reality and fantasy. These are all reasons to question his credibility."

Lastly, Kenna reminded jurors that it is not a crime to withhold information about a crime as Mrs. McLaughlin did for three months after her husband allegedly shot Robert Cushing, and that she had no possible motive to assist in the murder.

Kenna's last statement was, "On the night that Mr. Cushing died, her life died. She no longer has a life." *Authors note: In New Hampshire, withholding information about a crime is not a crime or violation. To be prosecuted for obstruction of justice or withholding evidence, someone with knowledge of a crime must lie to a police officer, either by fabricating or withholding information.*

****

Assistant AG Barbara Keshen began her closing statement by paying tribute to Robert Cushing Sr.

"He was a well-respected, well-loved contributor to society who cultured the soil, and not only the minds of his children, but also the minds of children he had taught. On June 1st, 1988, two men stood on opposite sides of a door. One man was contented and secure, the other was disillusioned and embittered."

Keshen argued that it was mainly because of his wife that Robert McLaughlin ever reached the Cushings door dressed in black, and with a plan to flee the scene afterwards.

"Too many questions remain unanswered about the shooting after McLaughlin's confession to the killing. Witnesses described a person at the scene who does not fit the description of the balding middle-aged McLaughlin. But the height and build match Susan McLaughlin. The evidence is overwhelming that there were two people there on the night Robert Cushing was killed."

Keshen also pointed out that three neighbors saw a person flee the scene, but while two of those descriptions were of a young blonde male, the third was of a young blonde male and a man dressed in black carrying what may be a gun.

"It is obvious, that this was Robert and Susan McLaughlin. The husband-wife team that killed Robert Cushing.

Keshen then turned to Robert McLaughlin junior who was in court and described him as a "Profile in Courage" for coming forward with testimony about his stepmother.

"Robert McLaughlin Jr. had little to gain from implicating his stepmother and admitting his knowledge. Instead, he faced the harsh scrutiny on his life and character that resulted."

"Bobby didn't get those details from the papers. They were factual and succinct details. He got them directly from the mouths of his father and stepmother. If Bobby McLaughlin fabricated his story just to get Sammi, why is there so much truth?"

"Susan McLaughlin not only chose to go along in this evil pursuit, she led the way."

****

With the end of closing arguments, Judge Temple gave the jury their final instructions which took more than an hour. Temple was very precise in detailing the charges against Sammi McLaughlin and the proof that must be shown to gauge the defendant's guilt. He clearly stated that "inferences and opening and closing arguments do not constitute evidence."

He then adjourned court, and the jury began to deliberate.

****

The jury broke deliberations on the second day to ask judge Temple a question concerning witness tampering and evidence that had been submitted during the trial. Specifically, the phone call to Beverly Russell from Sammi McLaughlin. Judge Temple advised the jury that they have to decide whether the conversation fulfills the charge of a witness to withhold information relevant to the case.

On the third day, both prosecuting and defense attorneys were at the court house speaking with members of the defendant and victim's families.

At 3:30 PM, the jury announced that they had reached a verdict on all charges and court was called to order.

****

After the jury entered the room and was seated, the foreman of the jury gave the clerk of courts their written decision on the charges which he in turn gave to the judge.

After reading the decisions on all charges, Judge Temple then asked, "Ladies and gentlemen of the jury, have you reached a verdict?"

The foreman of the jury stood and answered, "We have your honor."

"What find you?"

The foreman then read each charged followed by the jury's verdict; guilty on all charges.

There were numerous noises from the courtroom ranging from gasps, to clapping, to tears. Sammi McLaughlin showed no emotion.

Judge Temple immediately stated that she would receive the maximum sentence for conspiracy to commit murder of life without parole. The sentences for witness tampering would be heard later and most likely would be served concurrently.

Renny Cushing, who was acting as the family spokesman, was quoted in the Hampton Union as saying "There is no joy over the verdict for his family. I look forward for my family to move on with our lives."

Renny also showed empathy for Robert McLaughlin junior by saying, "We have both lost our fathers. It's clear my father's murder has left victims everywhere."

According to the Hampton Union, many people in town were not surprised by the verdict. However, Sammi McLaughlin's sister, Dianne Brown who was present at the court, said that, "She's innocent and I believe she is a victim. My siblings and I are all surprised at the decision because we all know Sammi and she is a kind person who would never hurt anyone. I think that the state used a lot of information that was hearsay and Bobby McLaughlin Jr. is mentally ill and his testimony should never have been used."

Defense attorney Bruce Kenna stated that he would immediately file an appeal.

Sammi McLaughlin continued to show no emotion and was immediately taken into custody by Rockingham County Sheriff's deputies, and transported to Rockingham County Jail. Later that week, she was transferred to her permanent home, the NH Correctional Facility for Women in Concord, NH, where she remains to this day.

****

Jury selection for the Robert McLaughlin trial was scheduled to begin on May 31, 1989, and the trial was slated to begin later that month.

Chapter 10
The Robert McLaughlin Trial

May 1989

During the month of May, Paul Twomey filed a number of motions in Superior Court. The first one was to have McLaughlin's confession to Rick Mathews be made inadmissible since he was under the influence of alcohol and Xanax. The defense attorneys also requested the exclusion of statements that McLaughlin made at Pease and Portsmouth hospitals because of Doctor-Client relationship.

Neither of these motions were allowed by Judge Temple.

Authors note: The Health Insurance Portability and Accountability act (HIPAA) wasn't passed until 1996. It would have been interesting to see the effects of that motion by defense if they were in effect in 1989.

****

A motion not related to the criminal portion of the case was for the state to pay for transcript costs since the account of Robert McLaughlin had insufficient funds. The money that was in that account from his meager savings and retirement was virtually gone. In a situation such as this, the defendant must show that he is indigent and the court will assign that defendant a public defender. While this was being done, Sisti and Twomey continued to represent McLaughlin and their fee would be paid by the state. Soon thereafter, the defense dropped a bombshell on the case.

****

May 17, 1989

On Wednesday May 17, there was a special pre-trial hearing before Judge Temple which his lawyers had previously requested. At this hearing was Barbara Keshen, Robert McLaughlin senior, Sammi McLaughlin, and her attorney, Bruce Kenna.

Under questioning from Paul Twomey, McLaughlin testified that his wife, Susan (Sammi) McLaughlin killed Robert Cushing Sr. According to the Hampton Union, it was an accusation that came after hours of tense questioning and it was not a statement that came easily from McLaughlin.

McLaughlin further testified that on the night of the murder before midnight, his wife woke and told him that she had killed someone in the Cushing home. McLaughlin said that he didn't believe her at first and then he looked out the window and saw police at the Cushing home.

McLaughlin further testified that his defense team had asked him to do this previously but he couldn't testify against his wife. He also stated that he had told another inmate his wife did it and also his brother and a bailiff.

Under further questioning from Twomey, McLaughlin said that Sammi had threatened to implicate him in the killing if he said anything. He also testified that earlier in the day, he told his wife that their marriage was over.

During Barbara Keshen's cross examination of McLaughlin, Keshen stated, "Your chivalry is very touching."

Attorney Twomey objected, the objection was sustained, and her statement struck from the record.

Attorney Bruce Kenna had no comment on the allegations but stated, "All I can tell you is that I can remember stories from way up north about wild animals who got caught in traps, and they chewed off their own leg because they were so desperate to get free."

June 4, 1989
Letter from prison

"Babe, I pray that they find you innocent. They've got to, you didn't kill Mr. Cushing, I did, and I know you said you'd never tell and you'd protect me.""

This was written by Sammi McLaughlin from jail to her husband who was in County jail. It was made public and immediately created an uproar.

Authors note: In the state of NH, all jailhouse correspondence is opened, read and possibly redacted by the facility prior to giving it to the inmate or allowing it to be sent.

June 6, 1989
Letter from Prison

"Hi Lady, I just got your letter and can't believe you gave me the "key." I don't know what to say except

"Thank you." I called Mark and Paul (McLaughlin's defense team) and gave them the letter. I feel so happy and yet so sad at the same time. Paul asked if we cooked this up to get me off. Do you believe that? He (Paul) said the AG's office would probably want our letters back and forth.

I don't know what is going to happen, but I will destroy all my letters from you before I give them up.

I Still Love You Susan!!
Very, Very Much
My Love-My Life-My Wife-My Soulmate
Your Husband
Love Always
xoxoxoxoxo

****

After receiving the letter that was "the key" from Sammi, Robert McLaughlin called his lawyers and presented the letter to them. The following day, the letter was presented to Judge Temple in another pre-trial hearing. This was attended by Sammi and Bruce Kenna. Kenna did not allow his client to testify citing the Fifth Amendment right to self-incrimination.

Judge Temple then ordered that Sammi McLaughlin's cell be searched and all correspondence inventoried and put in a sealed envelope, and remain sealed, until the following morning when it would be opened in court. A number of Sammi McLaughlin's family members were present and one member (to remain anonymous) said to a Hampton Union reporter that the letter might have been a fabrication that might have been introduced to win Robert McLaughlin's freedom, while Sammi's case is under appeal.

Copies of the correspondence found in Sammi's cell were given to both the defense and prosecution.

****

Everything about the murder of Robert Cushing, and trial of Robert McLaughlin continued to be bizarre.

The following week, Sisti and Twomey filed a motion in Superior Court that they be allowed to remove themselves from the case. In order to be removed as defense attorney's, they had to show "good cause." This was granted by Judge Temple who was also scheduled to be the presiding judge in the Robert McLaughlin trial. The trial was postponed indefinitely. Sisti and Twomey have never given a reason as to why they asked to be removed, citing Lawyer-Client privilege. Speculation still continues as to why. Since it came the week following the Sammi McLaughlin letter to her husband where she confessed that she killed Cushing, it is widely believed that may have been the issue since the correspondence may have revealed an issue of perjury that the defense attorneys would not be a party.

The Manchester Union Leader filed a motion that the "good cause" be released to the press. This was denied by Judge Temple. By Judge Temple granting Sisti's and Twomey's motion to be removed, this put the case in a state of limbo for many months, since new counsel would have to be sought and would have to familiarize themselves with the case.

Judge Temple temporarily assigned Michael Iacopino, a former public defender out of Manchester as defense counsel, and jury members who were already picked, were dismissed.

Another twist in the case occurred when Robert McLaughlin was moved from Rockingham County Jail in Brentwood to the NH State Prison for men in Concord, NH, in the second week of June. The only reason that was given was "for security purposes" with no further elaboration.

****

The unexpected continued in the trial.

Robert McLaughlin was eventually declared indigent and a public defender was sought to represent him. However, by the end of June, The NH Public Defender's office sent a letter to Judge Temple that they would not be able to defend McLaughlin because of a conflict of interest. When the Executive Director of the Public Defender's office, David Garfunkel, was contacted, he said, "Professional Ethics dictate that I cannot elaborate further on the conflict which prevents this office from representing Robert McLaughlin."

The reason that the Public Defender's office did not represent McLaughlin remains unknown and speculation was, and is, rampant to this day.

As a result, Judge Temple assigned Michael Iacopino as counsel and authorized a co-counsel after a motion was filed by Iacopino. Iacopino recommended Steve Shadallah, an experienced and competent defense lawyer from Salem, NH. This was approved by Judge Temple and their fee would be paid by the state.

Michael graduated from UNH in 1980 and obtained his J.D. Cum Laude from the Suffolk University School of Law. He was in the Public Defender's office from 1984-1987 and then established his own practice. Since then, he has continued to practice and is currently a senior partner at the office of Brennan and Lenahan in Manchester, NH.

Steve Shadallah graduated Magna Cum Laude from Boston University and also obtained his J.D. from the BU School of Law. He began his practice in Salem in 1979 and continues to this day. He is licensed in NH, Mass and Maine and his specialty is domestic issues and criminal litigation. He is a frequent speaker at bar association events on conducting trials and trial strategy in marital cases. He is consistently rated AV by Martindale Hubbell, the country's leading lawyer peer review service. Less than 5% of all attorneys in the country receive the AV designation by their peers.

An "AV" rating indicates that the attorney had reached the highest of professional excellence, and is recognized for the highest levels of skill and integrity.

****

Once assigned to the case, both lawyers in mid-July 1989, stated to Judge Temple, in a preliminary hearing, that they would not be ready for trial until mid-1990, because "of the daunting complexity of the case." Judge Temple

acquiesced to this though he stated he wished they would
be ready sooner. There was no objection from the state.

****

    There was never anything simple about the
McLaughlin case. In mid-July McLaughlin's defense team
filed a motion that he be moved since travelling to Concord
was time consuming and would add more to the fees that
they would charge the state. During the hearing, the
Rockingham County Jail's Chief of Security, William
Vahey, testified that he was informed by two State
Troopers that a current jail inmate told the Troopers that
McLaughlin was planning a prison break the night of
Thursday, June 15. According to the informant, someone
was going to leave a gun next to a jail fence for
McLaughlin to use in the escape. As a result, McLaughlin
was transferred to the maximum security prison in
Concord.
    After a recess, Judge Temple compromised and
ordered that McLaughlin be moved to Strafford County jail
in Dover, NH, and be put under strict surveillance. When
the jury selection and the trial began in March of 1990,
McLaughlin was moved back to Rockingham County Jail.
    There was no indication of whom was to leave the
gun for McLaughlin, and speculation remains to this day.

****

Jury selection for Robert McLaughlin began March 6 of 1990. It was a long, drawn out process involving 250 potential jurors that had to be vetted by the judge and both the defense and prosecution. Barbara Keshen and Michael Ramsdell were prosecuting the case for the state and Steve Shadallah and Michael Iacopino for the defense. By March 13, eleven members of the 15 person panel (12 jurors and 3 alternates) were selected. Judge Robert Temple also made a number of pre-trial rulings during this period. Most notable, was a motion to suppress the statements made by Susan McLaughlin to Robert McLaughlin Jr. when she admitted to helping his father plan and carry out the murder of Cushing.

He ruled: "The statements made by Susan McLaughlin discussed the roles that she and the defendant played in the killing of Robert Cushing. The facts of this case indicate that Susan McLaughlin's statements to Robert McLaughlin Jr. do carry with them substantial badges of reliability which indicate the trustworthiness of the statements."

To no avail, the defense argued that by allowing the statements denies McLaughlin the right to confront his accuser.

However, another pre-trial motion was a victory for the defense. Sammi McLaughlin's conviction as an accessory to murder would not be admissible. In addition, testimony over McLaughlin's alleged escape attempt would also not be admissible.

By March 21, jury selection was completed and the trial began. McLaughlin was pleading not guilty by reason of insanity, a surprising and significant change from McLaughlin's prior statements that it was his wife, Sammi McLaughlin, who shot and murdered Robert Cushing.

****

In his opening statement, Assistant AG Michael Ramsdell began by describing Cushing as a loving husband and father of seven children and McLaughlin as a divorced and disturbed senior Patrolman. He went on to state:

"To most appearances, he was a good cop, a cop's cop. But there was another side to him, a dark side. It was a very dark side.

"Robert McLaughlin had two confrontations with Robert Cushing. The initial resentment grew into an ugly hatred." Assistant Attorney General Michael Ramsdell also said in opening arguments, "Robert McLaughlin hated (Cushing) every time he looked out his window and saw him working in his garden or sitting on his back deck. He released that hatred on June 1, 1988."

"The state will prove beyond a reasonable doubt, that the defendant, Robert McLaughlin Sr., committed the crimes of first degree murder and conspiracy to commit first degree murder. The state will provide proof which will describe shadowy figures running from the scene of the crime in addition to admissions made by McLaughlin to his son, Robert McLaughlin Jr., and on two occasions from a fellow police officer and a NH state Police investigator."

Ramsdell also stated that: "It is the duty of the jury to decide whether he was suffering from mental illness that produced the murder. After you find Robert McLaughlin guilty, you must decide if he was suffering from mental illness and was responsible for the murder. The answer to that question is no, he was not suffering from mental illness and yes, he was responsible for the murder."

After the opening statement from Ramsdell, Judge Temple adjourned for the day in order to give the defense time to respond to Ramsdell's accusations.

****

In his opening statement, Attorney Shadallah readily admitting that McLaughlin fired the two shots that killed Robert Cushing. Shadallah also parroted Ramsdell when he stated:

"Attorney Ramsdell said that Robert McLaughlin has a dark side. He is correct. Yes, Robert McLaughlin does have a dark side, and he was driven to commit the killing; driven by psychosis, aggravated by drugs and alcohol.

Shadallah said the defense will rely on the testimony of a Plaistow Psychologist who will testify:

"That McLaughlin was a likely candidate for a psychotic episode."

Shadallah went on to say that he will:

"Present evidence of how Robert McLaughlin, who was then Robert Randall, accidentally short his best friend and was then so riddled by guilt, pulled a "sham" armed robbery so that he would be caught and punished."

He went on to say that the defense will also present evidence on how McLaughlin was traumatized by his 1973 shootout in Hampton Falls, and how he received no help and was unable to talk to anyone concerning the incident. This was exacerbated when McLaughlin was the first to respond to a gunshot murder the very next year.

Shadallah continued by outlining McLaughlin's difficult divorce which led to a suicide attempt, his anxiety attacks which led to sick leave for counseling in 1986, and how he was involved in yet another shootout during that time. The jury will also see the movie "Apocalypse Now," a violent and surrealistic film that McLaughlin was watching the night of the murder and that he referred to later in describing his motive.

Shadallah finished by saying:

"There were in fact two sides to Robert McLaughlin, just like Wizard of Oz who tried to portray himself as strong, secure and confident, but in reality, the real person, the man behind the curtain, was not."

****

The American system of criminal prosecution is an accusatorial system, meaning the government, after accusing the defendant must prove its allegations by an adversary process. An adversary process is one in which each side (the prosecution and the defense) presents its most persuasive arguments to the judge or jury.

In a criminal trial, the prosecution must prove that an individual is guilty beyond a reasonable doubt. The prosecution goes first, with cross-examinations by the defense, and then the defense may or may not present witnesses. On some occasions, if the defense feels the prosecution has not presented a good case, the defense may rest without calling any witnesses and ask for a dismissal of charges. In the event that defense has called witnesses, the prosecution may call rebuttal witnesses.

The trial had an additional twist. Since the defense was pleading not guilty by reason of insanity, the prosecution does not have to prove that the defendant was sane. The onus falls on the defense to prove insanity.

The trial began on Wednesday, March 21.

****

Just as in the Sammi McLaughlin trial, the first witness the prosecution called was Marie Cushing, the widow of Robert Cushing. She described how she was at home and was watching the Celtics game when she heard a knock at the door.

"He got up to answer the door when I heard two shots and then I watched my husband go up in the air, and then went backwards over the hallway table."

As she was saying this, she was in tears as were many of her seven children who were also in the courtroom. It was obvious to many that she was in shock after her husband was shot.

"Did you see anything else," Barbara Keshen asked?

"No I didn't, not until the police arrived."

While her testimony was short, it was poignant and it affected everyone in court. During her testimony, Robert McLaughlin looked down at his hands that were folded on the table.

"No further questions."

Attorney Shadallah did not have any questions on cross examination.

Judge Temple adjourned court for the day for the purpose of having the Jury tour the Cushing residence.

****

The prosecution's next witness was Bill Lally.

The questions for Bill were mainly about the scene and the steps he took during the night of the murder in addition to describing the shooting scene. He also explained a diagram of the entrance to the Cushing home to the jurors and spectators. Lally also showed jurors the screen door that fronted the Cushing home before the shotgun blasts that killed Cushing. The blasts clearly showed the two holes from the shotgun slugs that killed him.

As he was about to sit down, Attorney Ramsdell turned to Lally and asked, in what seemed to be an afterthought:

"One final question Detective Lally. Robert McLaughlin has been described as a cop's cop, and a model cop by many members of the police department and community. Does he look like a cop's cop now?"

This question took Lally completely by surprise since it was not a question that he and Ramsdell had gone over prior to his testimony. The court went very quiet.

Lally just looked at McLaughlin and said "No."

"No further questions your honor."

Shadallah and Iacopino had no questions for Lally.

****

Ramsdell next called Rick Mathews to the stand.
Questioning began by Rick describing his long friendship
with McLaughlin and then recounting the arrests of Robert
Cushing and Gladys Ring in 1975. It had been learned
after the arrest of Gladys Ring that she was going to testify
on Cushings behalf on his contested arrest the previous
month, and she thought that was the reason she was being
arrested. Mathews testified that neither he nor McLaughlin
had any knowledge of Ring's pending testimony in the
Cushing case.

Mathews also testified that after the Cushings began
the petition to get McLaughlin and he fired, both he and
McLaughlin received bomb threats and "acrid criticism"
from some members of the community.

Ramsdell then asked Mathews about the night of
August 26, 1988 after he received a call from Sammi
McLaughlin.

The rest of Mathews' testimony was exactly the
same as it was during the trial of Sammi McLaughlin which
detailed Sammi McLaughlin's call to Mathews, and Robert
McLaughlin's subsequent confession to Mathews.

Attorney Iacopino's cross-examination of Mathews
consisted of McLaughlin's physical and mental state. He
asked if it appeared that McLaughlin was out of touch with
reality. This was objected to by the state since Mathews
was not a psychologist. After the objection was sustained,
Iacopino asked Mathews of McLaughlin's appearance and
speech.

Mathews testified that McLaughlin was disheveled and his speech was rambling. It wasn't the Robert McLaughlin he knew.

****

The next witnesses were Mary Cheney and the Cushings next door neighbors, the Andersons. Their testimony was also similar to what they testified during Sami McLaughlin's trial; specifically that they saw what they believed to be a young male with slicked back hair in the vicinity of McLaughlin's house. In addition, Linda Anderson said she saw a man in black crossing the street while carrying a sack.

****

Colon Forbes's testimony was also comparable to his testimony during Sammi McLaughlin's trial.

Ramsdell also elicited some other information.

Forbes stated that McLaughlin had told him that his years in law enforcement had been typified by him being "screwed over" and he blamed the events of 1975 with the Cushings and Gladys Ring as being the beginning.

"His job ate him up," Forbes testified.

McLaughlin also described to Forbes how he would see Marie Cushing on her rear deck crying, especially after the Salisbury Chief's funeral which gave him severe guilt feelings. This made McLaughlin contemplate suicide which led in turn to his heavy drinking.

Forbes last piece of testimony was that he knew of McLaughlin also confessing to another trooper who was standing guard outside his room at Portsmouth hospital.

****

Trooper Richard Kelly was stationed both outside and inside McLaughlin's room at Portsmouth hospital while McLaughlin was being treated as a suicide risk and extremely high blood pressure after his confession to Colon Forbes on the night he was arrested.

Kelly testified that McLaughlin detailed the killing in detail to him while he was in his hospital bed.

"McLaughlin said that he wished that he could turn back time and that he wished he never did it. He stated that it must have been the alcohol and drugs."

McLaughlin also told Kelly that while he had been treated well during his statement, he was going to invoke his Fifth Amendment right against self-incrimination.

Kelly further testified that after his shift was over, he went to the Troop barracks and did a report on what McLaughlin told him. The following day it was determined by Mike Hureau that since it appeared that Kelly had established a rapport with McLaughlin, he would stand guard duty the next night also.

When Kelly was on duty the next night, he testified that McLaughlin once again opened up to him and stated that, "In all those years after Cushing tried to get him fired, it just ate away at him and he had to do something.

****

Robert McLaughlin Jr.'s testimony was no different from the previous trial, and if there was any doubt in anyone's mind that It was Robert McLaughlin Sr. who killed Cushing, it was put to rest. The defense team had little to ask the younger McLaughlin except they were able to elicit statements of his father's heavy drinking and disheveled mental state.

It was now the defenses turn to call witnesses.

****

McLaughlin's personnel file, including psychiatric consultations and treatment were presented in open court.

The defense called Dr. Thomas Lynch who treated McLaughlin beginning in January of 1986, when he was on stress leave from the police department.

Lynch's testimony was the longest and most involved to date. These shootings, according to Lynch, led to McLaughlin becoming withdrawn and suicidal. He testified how McLaughlin had been traumatized by a number of previous shootings he was involved in beginning with the accidental shooting of his best friend when he was fifteen, the shooting at Punky Merrill's gun store in 1973 and the shootout he was involved in with Joe Galvin in 1986. Lynch further testified that McLaughlin was prescribed Xanax in December of 1985 and in a January

1986 letter to Bill Wrenn, he explained his diagnosis of McLaughlin's panic disorder, and recommended a paid leave of absence from the police department which was granted. Dr. Lynch further testified that when McLaughlin has theses panic attacks, he may lose control. Within a couple of months of treatment, McLaughlin slowly returned to duty on a regimen that progressed from doing paperwork in the station, to being doubled with other officers in a cruiser, to patrol on his own. In another letter to Deputy Chief Wrenn in April, Dr Lynch wrote that "McLaughlin has done remarkably well" and he would continue to monitor his progress.

On cross-examination, Dr. Lynch stated that he had treated other police officers with similar disorders.

"Dr. Lynch, did any of those officers kill anyone?" Ramsdell asked.

"No they have not."

****

The following day, the defense called Dr. Rowan to the stand who was the former head of the state's secure psychiatric unit. Prior to interviewing McLaughlin, he reviewed all of McLaughlin's previous psychological reports and wanted to try and "flesh out questions" about McLaughlin's relationship with the Cushing family. Dr Rowan testified that McLaughlin felt the Cushing family was anti-authority or anti the Hampton Police Department.

"Dr. Rowan, why do you think McLaughlin targeted Robert Cushing?" Shadallah asked.

"Because he was close," was the only response.

At this point, the court was adjourned so the jury could watch the movie Apocalypse Now. The Hampton Union described this movie as a "surrealistic violent movie depicting fictional events of the Viet Nam War."

Dr. Rowan testified that McLaughlin told him that while he was watching the movie, he was drinking heavily while taking Xanax.

Dr. Rowan stated that "The message imparted to McLaughlin was something about being able to kill someone that would prove you're a man and be able to survive the job."

****

That afternoon, defense continued their questioning of Dr. Rowan. Rowan testified that one of the lasting effects McLaughlin had of the shooting at Punky Merrill's gun shop was a recurring memory of the smell of the burglar's blood. Dr. Rowan had met with McLaughlin at the Strafford County jail in February.

McLaughlin was later sued by the burglar and according to court testimony, his financial and material assets were frozen until the judge dismissed the case. This was particularly stressful for McLaughlin since he was always criticized by his first wife that he did not make enough money and he was just starting a family since his son Bobby Jr. was recently born.

Dr. Rowan's final testimony centered on the stress McLaughlin experienced when he was the first responder to the murder on Woodland Ave, and the residual guilt feelings from the murder of his best friend when he was fifteen.

"Dr. Rowan, what does this boil down too?" Shadallah asked.

"As a result of all these factors in his life, the stress and pressure had built up to a point where he was operating under the delusion that if he killed someone, he could survive as a police officer. A delusion was a symptom of an underlying psychosis."

"Doctor, can you define a psychosis?"

"It is a severe mental disorder in which thoughts and emotions are so impaired, that contact is lost with external reality."

"Would you say Robert McLaughlin was suffering from this on the night of June 1, 1988?"

"Yes sir."

"Thank you Doctor, no further questions."

On cross examination. Barbara Keshen asked Dr. Rowan a number of questions concerning Rowan's definition of insanity. She pointed out that the American Psychiatric Association's definition differed from Rowan's. She also sighted a report from Dr. Seemans, the doctor that Mathews took McLaughlin to the night he confessed, that McLaughlin "Appeared oriented, spoke well, and did not display any delusional thoughts or hallucinations."

****

The last psychologist called was Dr. Rick Silverman, who performed a number of tests on McLaughlin while he was at Strafford County jail.

Dr. Silverman testified that the various test he
administered showed that McLaughlin had an average IQ
of around 100 and that he "showed a very suppressed and
superficial control over his emotions." He went on to state
that McLaughlin "underestimated his psychopathology" or
attempted to minimize the problems in his life. He had an
inability to cope with the stress he was feeling, especially
on the job. Silverman stated that, "McLaughlin is an
individual who tends to hold emotions in."

Silverman's examination also ruled out any kind of
brain damage but he felt there were indicators of post-
traumatic stress syndrome similar to combat veterans.

On cross-examination, Barbara Keshen only asked
one question.

"Dr. Silverman, your examination of Robert
McLaughlin was over a number of days in February of
1990, which is over a year and a-half from the murder. In
your testimony, did you offer any opinion as to Robert
McLaughlin's mental state on June 1, 1988?"

"No ma'am."

"No further questions."

****

The last witnesses called by the defense were
members of the Hampton Police Department.

Skip Bateman said of McLaughlin, "In the 1970's,
Bob McLaughlin was the officer that everyone looked up
to. Bobby trained us without being asked and taught us
how to survive."

Bateman said he was one of a hand of close friends that McLaughlin had in the department and he (McLaughlin) got to know him as a patrolman and then a supervisor.

"Bobby took pride in being a police officer. As he called it, a grunt, he was the first person on the street and on scene."

Other testimony was concerning McLaughlin's personal life.

"His first marriage was tough and it was not a pleasant divorce. It led him to a half-hearted suicide attempt in 1978 that he rebounded from."

****

The other two officers called were Chief Mark and Deputy Chief Wrenn.

Chief Mark testified that McLaughlin was looked upon as a good officer from all members of the department and was always impeccable in his dress and actions on duty. Attorney Shadallah then had Chief Mark read multiple commendations that McLaughlin received over the years. In addition to the two shootouts he was in, where his actions were exemplary, he saved a man's life in a house fire he discovered by administering CPR.

Deputy Chief Wrenn echoed the opinion of other officers when he said that he thought McLaughlin was an excellent police officer.

"He always displayed common sense and he always seemed to have the right answer."

Wrenn also testified that he knew McLaughlin in 1978, and of his divorce and aborted suicide attempt.

With the approval of Chief Mark, Wrenn granted McLaughlin his stress leave with pay in 1986. This was a result, in part, of McLaughlin telling Wrenn that he felt he was losing control of himself and he was drinking heavily. Wrenn felt that this was the right decision siting McLaughlin's performance in the Galvin shootout in addition to Dr. Lynch's favorable report.

There was no cross-examination of any of the officers.

"Your honor," said Iacopino.

"The defense rests."

Judge Temple then adjourned for the weekend and prosecution indicated that they had only one rebuttal witness that they would call on Monday, April 2.

****

When Court resumed on Monday, the prosecution called Dr. Albert Drukteinis as a rebuttal witness to the three psychiatrists called by the defense. Dr. Drukteinis not only had his PhD/MD, but also his Juris Doctor. He specialized in forensic psychiatry.

Dr. Drukteinis testified that after a four hour interview and a number of psychological tests he administered, he concluded, that while McLaughlin was most likely in need of therapy, he was not criminally insane at the time of the shooting.

Dr. Drukteinis also testified that the state of NH does not recognize a standard for insanity. He, and others, have used the American Psychiatric Associations definition as a reference point in their diagnoses, and this definition excludes intoxication as a component of mental illness. Drukteinis said his conclusion indicated McLaughlin suffered from panic disorders, depression and alcohol abuse.

On cross-examination, Attorney Shadallah focused on his contention "that psychology is not an exact science" which was not disputed by Drukteinis.

Shadallah also pointed out that he thought that Drukteinis had a very narrow definition of insanity.

Lastly, Shadallah said while pointing out a paragraph of Drukteinis' report, "You're telling us that officer McLaughlin was lashing out at the Cushing family as a symbol?"

On re-direct by Keshen, Drukteinis stated that he thought McLaughlin's motive for killing Cushing was not a delusion or a fixed false thought, but a conscious decision.

Court was adjourned for the day and Tuesday, April 3rd was scheduled for closing arguments.

****

Barbara Keshen began her closing argument by criticizing Robert McLaughlin as a failure in his career and marriages, and "who was a cold, calculating murderer who tried to rationalize his problems by killing Robert Cushing."

"Robert Cushing was a wonderful family man who nurtured and cultivated his seven children and the students he taught for over 15 years. By contrast, Robert McLaughlin is a man who has known too much failure in his life and used Robert Cushing as a scapegoat. This killing was directed at Robert Cushing and it was well-planned with touches of using an untraceable shotgun, disguises, and destruction of evidence. Mr. Cushing's murder was not haphazard, it was not chaotic as defense would have you believe. It was precise, and it was successful. Robert McLaughlin is a man who had his wits about him on June 1, 1988.

Keshen went on to explain that, "The New Hampshire Attorney General's Office supports the insanity defense as a precept that society must uphold on behalf of the truly deranged. Robert McLaughlin doesn't deserve your pity or your compassion, but your contempt for using the insanity defense as an excuse for this well planned killing."

Keshen then added that since McLaughlin confessed to Sergeant Mathews and Detective Trooper Forbes on August 26, 1988, he then later testified under oath that his wife was the killer.

"This was later reversed when letters taken from Sammi McLaughlin's cell, admitted as evidence, that he coaxed her to accept the blame in a failed attempt to keep him from standing trial. Susan McLaughlin went from being his co-conspirator to being his sacrificial lamb. Can you imagine a more reprehensible act of betrayal?"

Keshen finished by saying, "Defense will have you believe that Robert McLaughlin was delusional the night of the murder of Robert Cushing. A delusion is a fixed lasting belief that dominates a person's life in a global way for a long period of time. It is not a twelve hour detour into La-La Land. Was he disturbed? Yes, but was he deranged, no."

****

Mike Iacopino delivered the closing argument for
the defense.

"The issues of this case goes beyond who done it or
where it was done. Please consider the proverb, 'you
should never judge someone unless you have walked a mile
in his shoes'. Place yourself in McLaughlin's forest green
uniform and patrolman's badge. He had an extremely
stressful career that involved two shootouts. Many officers
never draw their guns during their entire career."

Iacopino explained to the jury that intent and
premeditation must be proved in order to obtain a guilty
verdict for first degree murder, "and neither was present in
this shooting."

Iacopino continued, "What crime did Robert
McLaughlin commit? Ladies and gentleman of the jury, I
suggest to you that they were not first degree murder and
conspiracy to commit first degree murder. If you accept
the testimony of Robert McLaughlin Jr., Susan McLaughlin
premeditated and deliberated the murder. She was the one
who said, we need a plan."

Iacopino also pointed out to the jury that there was
not a specific target in the killing saying, "McLaughlin
could not see through the door and his previous admission
to a psychiatrist was that he wanted to shoot a Cushing."

Iacopino also explained to the jury that McLaughlin
tried to style himself as a Viet Cong guerilla after watching
the movie Apocalypse Now in order to find the ruthless
strength to survive into retirement. "This was not a rational
decision. It was a delusion in essence for his own self-

preservation that if he could kill a Cushing, he could survive. As Dr. Rowan put it, he had an actual accumulation of stressors that pushed him over the edge."

Iacopino then addressed the definition of insanity from the prosecution's rebuttal witness Dr. Drukteinis. "The state's definition of insanity from Dr. Drukteinis is so narrow, that prosecution would have you believe in order for him to be insane, Robert McLaughlin would have to be on all fours and barking at the moon for several months. Some may say Robert McLaughlin snapped, some may say he wigged out. They are all one and the same."

****

Judge Temple adjourned the court for the morning and it would reconvene after lunch at 1 PM. His instructions to the jury of six men and six women were virtually the same as he gave to the jurors at the Sammi McLaughlin trial.

Once again, Judge Temple was very precise in detailing the charges against Robert McLaughlin and the proof that must be shown to gauge the defendant's guilt. He clearly stated that "inferences and opening and closing arguments do not constitute evidence."

At 1:20 PM, court was adjourned and the jury began deliberations.

****

At 10:20 AM on Monday, April 9, the jury foreman, Paul Dolan, advised the bailiff that they had reached a decision. It had taken almost four days. The bailiff in turned notified Judge Temple who reconvened court.

Once again the bailiff took the written decision from the jury foreman and handed it to Judge Temple which he read. Robert McLaughlin and his two lawyers stood.

"Ladies and gentleman of the jury, what find you?"

"Your honor, we the jury, find Robert McLaughlin guilty of murder in the first degree."

Judge Temple sentenced McLaughlin to life in prison without the chance of parole which concluded the 14 day trial.

Robert McLaughlin slumped his shoulders and was immediately taken into custody and transported back to Strafford County jail, and then to Concord State Prison the next day.

The entire Cushing family was present for the verdict as they were for the entire trial. Members of the Cushing family were crying in the courtroom and they were all hugging each other.

Renny Cushing continued to act as the family spokesman when he said, "I, on behalf of the family, would like to express our thanks to the prosecutors, Barbara Keshen and Michael Ramsdell, to the personnel in the office of the NH Attorney General's office and to the state of New Hampshire itself for bringing the killers to justice."

Attorney's Shadallah and Iacopino stated that they would be appealing the verdict to the NH Supreme Court.

When Barbara Keshen was interviewed by the Hampton Union she stated that they were very pleased by the verdict.

"Technically speaking, it was not a very difficult case to prosecute since the defendant had confessed to the crime. It was a pretty straightforward case. Similar to the legal principle that a person is innocent until proven guilty, so it is a man is presumed to be sane until it can be proven otherwise. The burden of proof therefore rested with the defense, and it was obviously the decision of the jury that Robert McLaughlin was not temporarily insane."

****

The day after McLaughlin's conviction, Sergeant John Tommasi had just finished roll call at Salem, NH police department, prior to the four to midnight shift.

"I don't know if anyone has been following the Robert McLaughlin murder trial; he was found guilty yesterday and sentenced to life without parole. Something I want to pass on to you guys that one of the old-timers, Bill Campbell, told me when I was a rookie, 'When you lose your sense of humor in this job, it's time to call it quits'."

After a pause, "Okay, let's hit the road and don't anyone get hurt."

Chapter 11
Epilogue

There was very little about the murder trial of Robert McLaughlin that wasn't bizarre and it continued after the criminal trials were over.

The next twist came when Barbara Keshen, shortly after the trial, resigned from the Attorney General's Office, which came as a surprise to then Attorney General Steve Merrill.

What also came as a surprise, not only to Steve Merrill but to the Hampton Police Department, was when Barbara Keshen filed papers in Rockingham County Superior Court, on behalf of the Cushing family, suing the Hampton Police Department and Town of Hampton civilly in a wrongful death suit.

There were a number of people in the police department who believed that Barbara Keshen contacted the Cushings and was the one who suggested they sue the Town of Hampton civilly. This has never been confirmed.

The Town retained the services of the law firm of Wadleigh, Starr and Peters out of Manchester, NH. Their first action was to petition the court to have Barbara Keshen removed as the representative attorney for the Cushings.

Judge Temple once again entered the fray. In a pre-trial hearing, he ruled that there was an obvious conflict of interest, and Keshen was removed as the representing council. The civil case eventually went to trial but a settlement was reached by the third day of the trial between the Town and Cushing Family for an undisclosed amount.

****

Several days after the criminal trial the Hampton Union interviewed Chief Mark and Superior Court Clerk Ray Taylor on the cost of the trial. Chief Robert Mark estimated that the cost of the investigation and trial would be in the range of $250,000 (*about $520,000 in 2021 dollars*).

Ray Taylor identified many other costs in the trial such as the housing, transportation and feeding of the jury which he estimated would be in excess of $10,000. In addition, witnesses had to be paid for their appearance in addition to travel costs, and since McLaughlin was declared indigent, payment had to be made to his two attorneys, Iacopino and Shadallah, by the state.

This was confirmed by Shirley DeSalvo, the administrative assistant in the county attorney's office. She also stated that while witnesses are paid a moderate fee, expert witnesses can run from $100 to $1500 per hour.

The NH Attorney General's office did not provide any estimate of costs, but said they were significant.

What was not taken into account was the mental costs the Cushing family endured, in addition to all those involved in the investigation and the trial.

Those costs are most likely, still significant today.

Chapter 12
Where Are They Now

After exhausting two appeals to the Supreme Court, one in 1992 and another in 2000, Robert McLaughlin resigned himself to prison life. McLaughlin is 80 years old at the time of this writing and remains in jail. After being incarcerated in the Federal Correctional Institute at Lompoc, California, McLaughlin was transferred to Union Correctional Institute (also known as Raiford Prison) outside of Jacksonville Florida. He will occasionally write back to some of his friends who have kept in touch with him for over 30 years.

He has not attempted to obtain a pardon or parole since 2000.

****

Sammi McLaughlin remains in the NH prison for women since she was sentenced in 1989. While in prison, she sought, and was granted a divorce from Bob McLaughlin and changed her name back to Susan Cook. She is no longer called Sammi. She subsequently exhausted several appeals following her conviction and it appeared she had to resign herself to prison life, but she did not.

Upon entering prison, Cook attempted to contact her son. She wasn't successful until 2002 when she found out that her son, Ray McDaniels Jr. lived in Arizona with his girlfriend and four children. They started communicating by mail.

During a telephone interview with Seacoast Online, Ray McDaniels said he had always been curious about his mother and that until now he didn't know if she was dead or alive.

"Twenty-three years. That's a long time not to have a mom," Ray said. According to Seacoast Online, Ray wonders if his mother found him only to help in her quest for a pardon. "Maybe my mother has found God. I'm not into that, maybe she really wants to get to know me. It's very weird," McDaniels said.

When you receive a sentence of life without parole in NH, there still remains a glimmer of hope. If a prisoner can petition the governor's five person executive counsel for a hearing, she can then be eligible for parole or a pardon. She can also be pardoned by the governor.

In 2002, with the support of two New Hampshire women, she petitioned the executive council for a pardon. Sue Cook had previously gained the support of two advocates, Julie Normand and Cillia Clements who took up her cause. Clements, a school teacher and writer from Raymond, wanted to write a book about women in prison. She eventually sat down with six women in Goffstown, Cook being one of them. With their help, Cook applied for a pardon from then Governor Shaheen who was a champion of women's rights and battered women. Cook had claimed that she was abused when a child and also suffered abuse from her first husband and then Robert McLaughlin. The request sat on Shaheen's desk and then

Governor Craig Benson's after her. No action was ever taken.

After that failed they took her appeal to the executive council which was flat out denied. Since then, Cook has attempted three more times to get an executive council hearing, the most recent being July 10, 2019. The Council voted unanimously not to grant her a hearing. The associate attorney general at the time, Jeffery A. Strelzin, stated, "Justice and the law demands that the terrible consequences suffered by Robert Cushing and his family be fully recognized by the criminal justice system. The petitioner's (Cook's) guilty verdicts and sentences do just that, and should not be disturbed."

****

Marie Cushing did retire in June of 1988. After the death of her husband. She eventually moved from the family house and lived with some of her children while Renny bought the house.

Her background and kindness is reflected in her children's ardent beliefs and tolerance towards others. She passed away in February of 2021 at the age of 94.

Marie is lovingly remembered by her six surviving children: Robert Cushing, Jr. and his wife Kristie Conrad, Matthew Cushing, Kevin Cushing and his wife Kathleen (Hanson), Marynia Page and her husband Richard, Christine Rockefeller and her husband Dale, and Timothy Cushing and his wife Janet (Batchelder).

Marie Cushing did go to Ireland accompanied by her grandchildren. While there, she was very proud and

excited to show them the family house where her
grandmother was born.

****

Renny Cushing continues as an activist and
champion of liberal democratic causes in New Hampshire.
He bought his parent's house after his father's murder, and
lives there with his wife and three children. He is currently
serving his 7th term as a representative in the New
Hampshire State House and is also the minority leader. He
was appointed and continues to be the moderator of the
Winnacunnet School Board since 1993. He is a Justice of
the Peace and a member of National Writers Union-UAW
since 1994.

Renny was the founder and Executive Director of
the Murder victims' Families for Human Rights. From its
web site, MVFHR is an international, non-governmental
organization of family members of murder victims and
family members of the executed, all of whom oppose the
death penalty in all cases. The organization views the
death penalty as a profound violation of human rights.

During the 2019-20 legislative session, Cushing led
the effort in the New Hampshire Legislature to pass
legislation abolishing the death penalty in New Hampshire.
This campaign was so successful that he was able to garner
enough votes in the House and Senate to override Governor
Chris Sununu's veto. It was the only time that Governor
Sununu had a veto overridden.

Renny is an avid advocate and proponent of Black
Lives Matter and has voted in favor of doing away with
implied immunity for police officers.

In 2021, he was the commencement speaker at
Winnacunnet High school where he spoke about service to
the community and the importance of following your
passions.

He is currently battling stage 4 prostate cancer at
the time of this writing.

****

Barbara Keshen had been admitted to the bar in
1976. She served for five years as an Assistant Attorney
General before leaving and becoming a Public Defender in
1990. She continued to work as a public defender well into
the 21st century.

Along with Renny Cushing, she worked tirelessly to
abolish the death penalty in New Hampshire and she was
on the Board, and the Chair of the NH Coalition to Abolish
the Death Penalty. Barbara also served as the Legal
Director for ACLU-NH and continues to serve the
organization as a lawyer and advocate. Like Renny, she is
also an advocate of doing away with implied immunity for
police officers.

She continues to be an active member of the
Unitarian Universalist Church in Concord NH.

****

Rick Mathews retired from the Hampton Police Department in the 90's as a Captain. He lives in Southwestern Florida.

****

Bill Wrenn became Chief of Police in 1994 after then Police Chief, Robert Mark, retired. He subsequently retired from the Hampton Police Department in 2005 after a tenure of 31 years with the department. Shortly thereafter, he was appointed as the New Hampshire Corrections Commissioner by then NH Governor John Lynch. He retired from that position in 2017 and currently lives on the Seacoast with his wife.

****

Bill Lally continued a successful career in Hampton PD working another 14 years as a detective. He retired as a Lieutenant in 2002. He went on to become the Director of Training in the Lowell, Ma Police Department. While employed in Lowell, he concurrently served two terms as a Selectman in Hampton. He has since retired from the Lowell Ma Police Department and is living on the seacoast with his wife.

****

Tim Collins left the Hampton Police Department in 1988 as a full time officer but remained active as a part-time officer. He continued in Law Enforcement in the NH Probation Department until 2004. In those intervening years he earned two Master's degrees, one in Public Administration and the other in Education. In 2004, he became a teacher at Winnacunnet High School. At the time of this writing, he still teaches at the High School and patrols the streets of Hampton, NH as a part-time officer along with John Tommasi. They are frequently seen doubled in the Paddy wagon on patrol.

Tim lives with his wife and children on the NH seacoast.

****

John Campbell retired from the Hampton Police Force in 2000 and still remains active as a Special Police Officer in Hampton. He still lives in Hampton and remains happily married for over 40 years to his high school sweetheart Leslie. He has remained a close friend of John Tommasi since High School and they frequently work together.

****

Shawn Maloney retired from Hampton PD in 2006 as a detective Sergeant and he resides in the seacoast area.

****

Colon Forbes retired from State Police as a Captain in 1999 after a 23 year career. He then worked as an investigator for an insurance company where he was promoted to a supervisory position. In 2009, he was appointed as the Director of Professional Standards for the NH Department of Corrections by Commissioner Bill Wrenn. His duties included all aspects of the Department's Investigations Bureau, Hearings Office, Polygraph Unit, and Audit section.

He retired in 2017 and currently lives with his wife in the seacoast area.

****

John & Joe Galvin are retired from the Hampton Police Department. John retired in 2009 and Joe in 2014. Both are active as part-time officers during the summer months at Hampton. You can see them on weekends patrolling Hampton on the department's two horses. They both live with their wives in the seacoast area.

****

Linda Anderson survived the rape and attempted murder on her life. She continued her nursing career, subsequently married, and had three children. For the rest of his career, Bill Lally continued to work the case on and off. He was able to find patterns of similar cases in Vermont and California, however, none of the victims survived. In 2009, a black man by the name of Valentine Underwood was arrested and brought to Massachusetts for prosecution by the US Marshalls. At the time of his arrest, he was serving two concurrent life sentences in California for murdering two woman in 1991. He had been found as a result of DNA evidence.

Underwood, when he committed the California murders, was a marine who had recently returned from the Gulf War. He was dubbed by the California press as the "Marine Corp Killer." He was tried and convicted in California and is currently serving a life sentence in California.

When he abducted Anderson in 1988, he was working for a construction firm in New England.

Underwood was convicted on May 19, 2014, twenty six years to the date of the rape and attempted murder of Anderson in a Massachusetts superior court in Essex County. If he ever gets paroled from California, he will then serve 30-40 years in Massachusetts.

Before handing down the sentences, the presiding judge, Howard Whitehead commended the victim, a key trial witness, for her "never give up attitude" that saved her life when she was attacked. He noted what happened to her in 1988 is "every woman's nightmare."

At the trial, Anderson addressed Underwood directly and said, "Valentine Underwood, you tried to kill me in many ways, but you didn't and you are now being held accountable."

Underwood was 52 years old when convicted in Massachusetts. It is safe to say that he will spend the remainder of his miserable life behind bars.

Bill Lally testified at court against Underwood and the guilty verdict provided closure. It was significant closure for Linda Anderson who also testified at the trial. *Authors note: Linda Anderson is a pseudonym. Rape victims are rarely identified by the press and police.*

****

Mark Sisti continues to practice law. The offices of Sisti and Twomey are located in Concord, NH. If there is a high profile case in New Hampshire, he is usually involved. One of his most famous cases was the defense of Pam Smart. Mark is also a fellow in the American College of Trial Lawyers and has been named to the "NH Best Lawyers" list for the past ten years in the areas of white-collar criminal defense and non-white collar criminal defense. Mark has been involved in thousands of jury and bench trials, and represented individuals in every county in New Hampshire at every level, including over 100 individuals charged with homicide. He has also appeared before the NH Supreme Court.

****

Bruce Kenna also continues to practice law. After the McLaughlin trial, he became a First Assistant U.S. Attorney for New Hampshire. He currently has a practice in Manchester, NH with Kevin Sharkey.

****

Mike Hureau retired from State Police in 2003 after thirty one years of service. He then became the supervisor bailiff of Rockingham County Superior court. In 2016, after the passing of Mike Downing, the High Sheriff of Rockingham County, Mike was appointed to that position where he served for four years until his mandatory retirement at age seventy. Mike lives in Rockingham County with his wife.

****

Tom Ferris eventually left Salem, NH and became an agent with the Drug Enforcement Agency and participated in operation Snowcap in Bolivia. He retired after 25 years and remarried. He and his wife are currently living in northern Massachusetts.

Mark Cavanaugh also left Salem, PD, and joined the Naval Criminal Investigative Service. He returned to Salem after five years preferring to be a street cop than a federal agent. He retired after twenty years, as a detective Sergeant, remarried, and is currently living in southwestern Florida.

The Salem PD, M street boys still get together for choir practices along with Paul Marchand, Randy Marcin, Fred Rheault and Roger Beaudet.

Authors note: Operation Snowcap was a four year operation where certain DEA agents underwent Special Forces training, and then teamed up with Army Green Berets who in turned teamed up with the Umopar, the Bolivian National Police. They then went into the Bolivian jungle, established base camps and went on search and destroy missions for cocaine labs. This is highlighted in the authors other book, Danger Zone, which can be obtained on Amazon. Operation Snowcap, though highly successful, was terminated by the Clinton Administration in 1993.

****

Bob McLaughlin from a 1970's photo. He is in the first
Row, first officer on the left.

Sammi &Bob McLaughlin after their arrests.

Pictures of the Cushing grave. Notice the porous texture of the headstone. In the picture on the left, there are coins that have been left on the grave. This is a tradition of the armed forces. This lets the family of a deceased serviceman or woman know that somebody stopped by to pay their respects. A penny means a person visited. A nickel means that you and the deceased soldier trained at boot camp together. A dime indicates that you served with the soldier. A quarter means that you were there when that individual was killed. There are also stones on the grave, unlike flowers, rocks are permanent, so they remain on the grave as a memento forever, and symbolize that you will never forget the deceased.

Pictures of demonstrations by the Clamshell Alliance at the Seabrook Nuclear power plant. Notice the incorrectly spelled sign on the right.

Valentine Underwood as he appeared in Salem, Ma
Superior Court in 1988.

Bill Wren on the left, Sandy Lally and Bill Lally at Bill's
retirement party.

Made in United States
North Haven, CT
13 December 2021

12701690R00143